TO FEWER DAYS THAT SUCK

DITCH UNHEALTHY HABITS
UNZIP A *Happier You*

DEBORAH MALLOW
YOUR RAY OF SUNSHINE

Dedicated To Our Dreams.

Take Ownership Of Challenges.
Be Your Own Hero!

Wollam Works Publishing, New York

Library of Congress Cataloging-in-Publication Data

Name: Mallow, Deborah—Author.

Title: 6 Steps To Fewer Days That Suck: Ditch Unhealthy Habits Unzip A Happier You / Deborah Mallow

Description: New York: Wollam Works Publishing, [2024]
First Edition, October 2024 | Printed in the United States of America

Identifiers: LCCN 2023911760
ISBN 9798218222307 [hardcover]
ISBN 9798218222314 [paperback]

LC record available at https: //lccn.loc.gov/ 2023911760

Subjects: Self Help–Personal Growth | Happiness | Esteem | Success | Self-Management–Stress Management | Habits

This book is available in print, as an ebook, and as an audiobook. It can also be purchased in bulk. To inquire, please email: info@thedailydecisions.com.

Join Me At: www.thedailydecisions.com/inspire

USE THE LINK OR SCAN THE QR CODE:

Receive Complimentary Worksheets, Checklists, And Feel-Good Activities Designed As Companions To This Book.

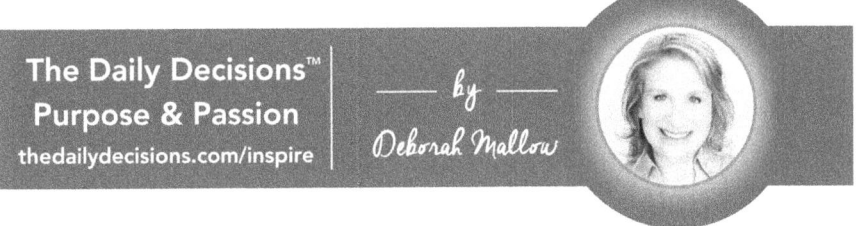

The Daily Decisions™
Purpose & Passion
thedailydecisions.com/inspire — *by* — *Deborah Mallow*

Deborah's Positive Energy Club, The Daily Decisions™ Welcomes You.

Personal empowerment with a creative, fun approach.
We stay focused on your happiness, contentment, and best life.

ATTRACT THE LIFE YOU WANT!

Table of Contents

Introduction

At ten years old, winning at the game of tetherball was my life's focus. Always having been smaller than the average person, I was determined to compete with the best in this sport. Practicing all summer paid off. From that point onward, I began setting goals for myself.

While I never felt gifted in any specific skill, I didn't let that hold me back. Goal setting in my youth provided the framework I needed to work through struggles, deal with difficult people, and address problematic situations in order to fulfill future accomplishments and gain personal success.

Without realizing it, I experienced firsthand that by having determination and self-belief, taking action, providing effort, and following through, I had the secret ingredients necessary to achieve my objectives. As a result, I gained recognition.

Unwilling to sail through life aimlessly, crafting a plan has been my key focus ever since my tetherball days. I ask you: Why feel stuck? A square peg won't fit into a round hole—find your fit.

This book is a product of my process. It started as my own guidebook, and evolved into a mission to teach how to create a positive mindset, build confidence, and live a happier, more productive, purpose-driven life. This is an invitation to join in.

A future goal is to introduce my life skills program to children and teens to help them develop self-trust, fight negativity, and empower their inner strength as a means of becoming kinder adults—successful not just monetarily, but mentally happy too.

Adversity is part of life. Resilience, embracing self-belief, and cheerleading ourselves on is a ticket to thrive.

Discipline is a key ingredient to muscle through hard work.

Anecdote:

The process of writing this book was a labor of love. Life got in the way. Even though I stopped and started, the desire never left me, gnawing at my insides until the last word was written.

I offer up what began as my personal guidebook, with questions that kept me on track, lined pages to write notes, and action items to improve and stay positive.

My purpose is to share pep talks, stories, and tips, as motivation for anyone who wants to make the necessary changes to improve their life.

Step 1: The Decision

It starts with an idea, and now it's time to take action—fix bad habits, secure self-belief, and trust that it's possible to reach your potential and turn dreams into reality. My goal is that my lessons inspire you.

Is there something you want to achieve? Then focus on these words: *Yes, I can*. Push forward. Work to break through the obstruction; commit to the transformation.

Key Takeaway:

Welcome your best life. Resist the excuses, self-reflect, adjust, and pursue your path ahead. Remain engaged, create opportunities, learn, and grow. Why let fear decide your destiny? Lead your way.

No more complaining! Summon up a positive mindset and repeat: *I'm doing this for me.*

Take a moment to reflect before letting life's distractions interfere with passion. Fight an inclination toward complacency and achieve what's in your heart. I found that making a plan and seeing it through ended my living with regrets.

Choose Your Own Path

Why just stick your toe in the water?
Instead, jump in and make a splash.

The Commitment

Life isn't a dress rehearsal. Choose your direction. Believe in yourself. Every day is a gift to be cherished and lived to the fullest. Make the decision: Instead of accepting a life by default, actively create it. Take charge and be consistent. Your destination awaits.

Why just imagine it? Act! Get in the habit of doing a little each day. Craft your desired future and work to turn those dreams into reality. My experience proves that effort links to results.

Make the choice: Let go of jealousy—it depletes energy. My rule is to replace it with curiosity. Follow a path of purpose fueled by passion. Personal pride is a bonus.

You hold the power to build inner strength and self-confidence. Staying true to your heart often leads to greater fulfillment.

Ask yourself: What's calling you from deep inside? Victory means something different to each of us. Create time to achieve your vision—imagine how good it will feel to live it.

Reflect: What if Einstein, Serena Williams, or Jobs had given up pursuing their personal best when facing a challenge? A new road may forge a better direction. Grow! Why stagnate?

Key into this visual: Once on the path, like a snowball gaining momentum, you become unstoppable. Align with that picture—trust it's possible. Today is the day to get started. Stop fighting against yourself. Why should fear be an obstacle?

Guiding steps: Positivity and self-belief are helpful in achieving your desired outcomes. 1. Shed insecurity. 2. Embrace confidence. 3. Take action. My mantra inspiring hope: *Dream it, make it happen, and live it.*

 *Start Now*: **TAKE THE LEAP!**

Choose your Daily Decision journal—use a notebook, a writing app, or the lined pages in this book. Keep all your thoughts, ideas, and notes in one place.

Make it important: Be accountable! Work on dismissing the negative voice from creeping in. Why let that be a deterrent? Firmly say: *I can*. Kindle the fire and cultivate your life. Intention is the driver; dedication and belief, the fuel.

Strategic approaches: Strive, accomplish, and thrive. Are you just going through the motions each day? Life is short; living with gusto, not apathy, aids progress. Promise not to be complacent—reach for your potential. Make that your final decision!

Think about this: Challenges deliver growth and confidence.

In a Nutshell

* Live determined; don't fear change. Make today count.

* Create your own path; walk it with curiosity, not dread.

* Grow! Don't give up, no matter the adversity you face.

Align With Your Destiny

When you stop making excuses,
you open the door to living more fully.

————————

The Commitment

Hey you, stop blocking my sunshine. Why allow anyone to decide your future? Instead, be the director. Keep a clear objective in mind, problem-solve, develop a strategy, and then claim the golden ticket. Life is yours to live, not someone else's picture of what it should or could be. Step up and select the best choice.

————————

Do you know who's in the driver's seat of your life? Is it you?

If your days are spent like a hamster in a cage on an endless wheel—escape. Commit to fulfilling your aspirations. Why just exist and limit your results? Make room for grander plans.

1. *Seize the opportunity*: Take control of your destiny; don't let it be chosen for you or simply happen. Pledge that daily responsibilities won't become excuses to let go of those innermost desires. Stop being a box-checker in your own life.

2. *Promise*: Whenever you say you're tired or that you have no time, make an edit in that moment. Come up with new phrasing, get revved up, and right then take a small action.

3. *Aha*: Confidence in your ability is a key to success. Accomplishment lifts self-esteem and feeds the soul.

Knock, knock. Who's there? Your life! Be there to answer. Whether you view destiny as a matter of choice or fate, commit to taking action—be present and accountable.

Create self-proof: Make what seemed impossible, possible. 1. Keep on learning. 2. Give yourself room to brainstorm. 3. Repeat Wayne Gretzky's words: "You miss 100% of the shots you don't take." 4. Mix tenacity, determination, and effort.

 *Start Now*: **FLIP THE SCRIPT!**

Use this mantra to tap into an abundance mindset: *There is plenty of room for all ideas.* Take fifteen minutes to set up a special space, a peaceful spot to dream, grow, and focus on yourself and your plan.

Visualize your future; plant the seeds and nurture, nurture, nurture. Lessons learned provide valuable knowledge. As achievements blossom, personal pride brings energy to persist. Cheerlead onward! Invite friends and family to root you on. Change direction as necessary, and keep on keeping on.

The concept that *daily decisions determine destiny* reminds me of the artist Grandma Moses. Her love of art began in childhood, and that passion never left. In her seventies, she took up painting, and remarkable success followed. Let magic happen! Sync with your best life, no matter your age.

In a Nutshell

* Challenge yourself: Stop box-checking your days away.

* Make time—take the shot and align with your destiny.

* Step up! Life is waiting—be your own cheerleader.

Make A Pact With Yourself

Today is the beginning of the future ahead;
become all that you aspire to be.

———————

The Commitment

*Start fresh: Figure out what you really want to accomplish. Commit
to it, sign in, and reach your full potential. Instead of holding back,
fight through the struggles, and see your vision to completion.*

———————

How many times do we make and break New Year's resolutions? With the best of intentions, many of us find ourselves at square one, ringing in the next year. Life gets in the way.

When acknowledging the lack of progress—same routine and bad habits—it's easier to rationalize why nothing has changed. Here's the question: *Do excuses make us feel better?*

It may help to ponder whether justifying our decisions is really just fear talking. Fear's job is to protect us from doing anything perceived as dangerous; unfortunately, it hinders progress.

It's instinctively natural in the animal kingdom (yes, we're included) for fear to kick in and warn us when danger lurks. No matter how convincing our minds' arguments are, it's unlikely we'll be in harm's way face-to-face with a wild boar. If so—run.

Permission to self: Although a passage may be uncharted, dismiss, then thank fear for its warning, and faithfully vow to continue moving toward your destination, but remain aware.

Picture this: Jim Carrey inspires me to believe that with effort and self-belief, it's possible to achieve what's in our hearts. His youth wasn't easy. The family lived in a minivan after his dad lost a so-called *safe* job. This gave Carrey the incentive to take a risk and do what he loved. Visualizing success as an actor/comedian, he wrote a promise check to himself for ten million dollars. The check reinforced his dream, and he persevered. In time, he scored a movie deal for that very amount. Manifestation at work.

 *Start Now*: **CHANGE THINGS UP!**

Take twenty minutes today to adjust your thinking. Agree to stand with your objectives, not the deterrents. Begin with: My dream is more likely than my fear because_____.

Commit, continue, and muster up the discipline to finish what you start. Dreaming is just the beginning. Say: *Yes, I will.* Make the decision to see what's on the other side of those rough patches. Envision what *could be* this time next year.

Mistakes are part of life; learning from them is essential for growth. Bravely refuse to flee from fear or hard work, instead, dive in. Challenges can make us our worst enemies or best allies.

Life whisks by. Days melt into weeks, months, and years. We all have the same twenty-four hours to manage our time. A forever mantra: *Today, I make a pact to live life to the fullest.*

In a Nutshell

* Make a pact with yourself: Do the work; follow through.

* Gather the discipline, start, push forward, and continue.

* Do what's in your heart; stop rationalizing, no excuses.

Design Your Life And Achieve Your Potential

The difference between the unattainable and the attainable is rooted in your perseverance.

The Commitment

No matter how many times you detour while pursuing a master plan, the key is to get back on the path and keep going. Harness your energy, collect strength, convert to self-belief, and proceed with extra willpower to stay on course.

Do you really want to achieve *your* objectives? Summon up swagger, move forward, put in the effort, and fulfill *your* goals. Why let obstacles become a reason to lose hope?

A secret to get moving: Live with purpose! Trigger memories of being engaged and feel the rush of adrenaline. In that flow state, thoughts start percolating and what appeared daunting becomes easier.

The hardest part is often taking the first step toward a desired outcome, and then being consistent. Stay positive—ambition is in our control. Imagine the result and take action.

I think of it this way: If the idea remains in the back of your mind, stop wasting time procrastinating and tackle it. Make an even trade. One approach is no more uncomfortable than the other, but only one leads to achieving true potential.

Own up to your fears. How? 1. Challenge negative thinking. 2. Prepare mentally. 3. Stay determined! Bravery, self-motivation, and persistence can be mastered with practice.

The image of success and achievement is unique to each of us, and sweat equity serves as the equalizer. Strive for your victory. Trust in yourself and repeat this mantra: *I'll persevere!*

 *Start Now*: **TAKE THE LEAP!**

It's empowering to first test out an idea in your mind. Take fifteen minutes, imagine your ideal life, and immerse yourself in that picture. Write down a summary of the vision. Ready, set, go! Start by doing one thing.

What if our mistakes are opportunities in disguise? I choose to rename the word failure, and call it education. Learn, grow, and accept the lessons received as a gift to advance with more insight.

Here's a solution: Recall past successes and remember how it felt to see the impact of your work. This feeling is the stimulus for future aspirations. Twists, turns, and setbacks happen along the way; believe in your worth and emerge stronger and wiser.

Kevin Systrom and Mike Krieger developed a social sharing app called *Burbn*, which struggled to gain traction. Realizing that users preferred the photo-sharing feature, they listened, pivoted, and transformed it into *Instagram*. Make your opportunity!

In a Nutshell

* Rise to your potential; live with purpose—feel the pride.

* Don't let a glitch block the way—aim for your goal line.

* Just start: Replace fear with positivity and dedication.

Believe In Yourself

Setbacks are part of life; resilience is how we thrive. With determination and effort, we can master new skills.

_____

The Commitment

Promise to push aside thoughts that could derail your plans, as they can crush the chances to see what's possible. Choose to embrace confidence, invest time, set intentions, and construct the framework.

_____

The enemy of our passions often consists of self-imposed constraints that inhibit our activities, lead us to justify unfinished projects, or cause us to succumb to angst and self-sabotage. Getting to the root of it is tricky, but beneficial for breaking the cycle.

Feeling unfulfilled is a clue. It lets you know that your fire is still burning. Why not use that bottled up frustration to urge you forward? When you're driven by passion, procrastination can't become the nemesis. Why throw away the possibilities?

Memo to self: I'm inspired by people whether young, old, or in between, who are willing to overcome obstacles in pursuit of their dreams. Not everything works out—simply trying can help build confidence and offer insights for future success.

Picture this: Arianna Huffington's self-belief was integral in overcoming rejection. Over thirty publishers turned down her second book before she finally secured a deal. She persevered and later co-founded *HuffPost*. Arianna's venture, *Thrive Global*, evolved from personal struggles. Her healthy, science-based strategies for fighting stress and burnout had an impact on my transformation.

Remember: It is so important to keep hope and faith alive.

When confidence is low, think of Eleanor Roosevelt's words: "No one can make you feel inferior without your consent."

Think of bumps in the road as learning tools and clues guiding you toward that successful outcome. Each day, focus on being positive. Lift your voice and say this mantra: *I believe in myself!*

 *Start Now*: **DITCH THE HABIT!**

To quit the goal abandonment habit, call or write one trusted friend today. Enlist them as a confidant, ask for their support, and share your commitment and proposal. Set up time for progress updates.

Surround yourself with people who believe in you. Distance yourself from destructive individuals. Agree not to give in to anyone who says *you can't*, without offering evidence.

Cultivate self-esteem and hold yourself accountable. If you experience a setback, simply recommit, and keep going.

Self-trust and a confident outlook are anchors that help when setting goals and working to accomplish them. My conclusion: With over eight billion people in the world, fight the impulse to listen to the few who try to tear you down.

In a Nutshell

* Team up with confidence. Call out: *I believe in myself!*

* End self-sabotage; break out of your own straitjacket.

* No matter your age: Learn, step up, and forge ahead.

Breathe Into Your Dream

The best way to create a better future is to make the decision to work toward it.

———————

The Commitment

When feeling overwhelmed, take a breath and a time-out. Why allow emotions to get the better of you or be a reason to give up on your goals? Make the choice to turn each day, week, and year into the best it can be. Objectives are only attainable if worked on and nurtured.

———————

Has the exhaustion of life gotten you down? Capitulating to laziness with a little bit of irrational fear sprinkled on top can do a number on your drive—refuse entry. Trust your abilities.

1. *Ask*: Why resort to panic, get caught up in the minutiae of the moment, and then fall into a trap, claiming lack of time for anything other than the daily routine? Make room for what's important and the opportunity to have a fuller experience.

2. *Personal struggle*: Identify and create time to change what's needed—a job, family, and commitments shouldn't be barriers. Pay attention and focus on the internal signal. Breathe into your dream steadily; form a habit. Don't shortchange yourself.

3. *Tailor the inner dialogue*: Why not rewrite your history, take control, and shift? Give yourself permission to start. Resist phrases like one more minute, one more hour, or I'll do it another day. Welcome this mantra: *No time like the present!*

Consider whether you'll regret denying yourself a chance to try. If the answer is, *I don't care*, then switch direction. Otherwise, toughen up and make it a priority to go after your objectives.

Rejection is a part of life. *The Beatles* were told guitar groups were losing popularity; comedian Jerry Seinfeld froze his first time on stage and was booed off. Why give up?

 *Start Now*: **FLIP THE SCRIPT!**

Use a few minutes to retrace your perfect daydream. Feel good about your goal! Pluck a doable slice and address it today. Do a serving daily. Bon Appétit!

Taking action is more productive than making another excuse. Push through challenges. Recognize and dismiss any demons; release the inner combat. Pursue your ambitions and gain satisfaction. When you follow a desire and act, a routine can develop.

Here's a solution: Research suggests the brain seeks patterns. Use this insight to help create positive habits that stick. Form a new routine by breaking large goals into smaller ones. Measure progress, be consistent, make it fun, and reward achievements.

Tip: Celebrating momentum along the way is inspirational, inviting action and bringing you closer to your dream. Think about this: *Why compromise your life's vision?*

In a Nutshell

* Shake off angst, panic, and laziness—make a change.

* Praise and celebrate achievements; live your dreams.

* Direct your life: Take charge—create positive habits.

Never Limit Yourself

Turn fear into fuel. Own your confidence
and be someone you can admire.

The Commitment

Believe you are capable. Attitude and outlook play a part in an outcome. Self-confidence can be a powerful weapon to combat a negative mind. Prevent the battle within and lean on trust. Release self-doubt.

Why do we sometimes buy into self-limiting beliefs, accepting that our goals are out of reach? If *you* believe *you* can't, *you* may not try. Don't play fortune teller.

Avoid setting yourself up to ask: Am I limiting myself? Think of it this way—if you dismiss an idea before it develops, and don't pursue it, someone else might.

Fix your eyes on the prize: Take a shot. Stop wondering what could've been—focus on what's possible. Put in the effort to work on *your* objective and earn *your* reward.

Add self-worth: Why adopt a defeatist attitude, convinced that you're not good enough? Instead, reflect before trusting naysayers, try anyway, build fortitude, and rinse and repeat.

Tip: Chart your life. Thoughts and actions are a choice. Echo Leon Brown's words: "It all begins and ends in your mind. What you give power to has power over you, if you allow it."

Now consider Henry Ford's quote: "Whether you think you can or think you can't, you're right." Embrace *I can!*

We all have days that are grueling and leave us spent. Take a break, reenergize and boldly continue. Endorse the adage: "Rome wasn't built in a day."

> Picture this: Over the years, I discovered my own capabilities by hitting goals people said were unreachable. I was told that I couldn't get a design director job because I was too young, secure a licensing contract because I wasn't famous, or become a top sales rep because I hadn't done it before. This fueled my refusal not to limit my choices. Yup, trying anyway is worth it.

 *Start Now:* **CHANGE THINGS UP!**

> **Find a quiet spot, then reflect on a fearless moment when you were a child. Did you climb a tree or sled down a steep hill? See if you can hold the feeling for a full five minutes, and think about what you cherish.**

Side with positivity; keep striving toward your vision. Patience, experimentation, and learning from mistakes are important parts of the process. Remember to take pride in your progress.

Work with consistency. Why be restrained by your thoughts, or anyone else's? Limitation is a dead end. A mantra to hug: *I am my own person. I choose to live my best life.*

In a Nutshell

* Nix self-limiting beliefs: Trust yourself; own your power.

* Remain positive and reflect before heeding naysayers.

* Be courageous and steadfast—work at your pace.

No More Excuses

Wasted time is something you can never get back.

_____

The Commitment

Are you about to make an excuse? Take a moment to reflect and reverse your thinking. Recognize what you're doing, and confront the weakness to give in. Don't allow yourself that minute to slack off.

_____

Are you the queen or king of rationalizations, a procrastinator extraordinaire? Would you agree that many of us could get an A in the *coming up with excuses* category? Is I'll do it another time a familiar saying? It comes down to priorities.

If you don't keep yourself in check, it's easy to be dragged down by everything that's annoying and upsetting. Is this a frequent struggle, a vicious cycle? Do you complain, but never change? Your answers expose the truth. Revision is a decision.

1. *You hear me, self?* A key is to overcome obstacles that prevent forward movement and grasp your heartfelt dream.

2. *Run interference*: Giving up may appear easier at the moment. Ask yourself: Is it? Defending less-than-optimal options can undermine your passion. Cop-outs are stealing your applause. Why continue an unproductive habit?

3. *Take an honest inventory of your excuses:* Do you blame your commitments, fear of failure, or judgment? Is it guilt, shame, or procrastination? Consider these difficult questions.

4. *Ask*: Who's judging you? Don't let an imagined evaluation become a barrier. Put on your body armor and add tenacity.

Start Now: **DITCH THE HABIT!**

Take half an hour, open your calendar, block out time to work on what you want to achieve, and strive to be consistent. Identify anything that disrupts your day or serves as an excuse, and remove those distractions.

Picture this: Bad things happen—self-belief matters. Successful actor, writer, producer, and director Tyler Perry suffered family abuse throughout his youth. He was kicked out of high school and attempted suicide, yet his past didn't define him. He overcame criticism through hard work and resilience.

Reminder: Bet on yourself—you can change the trajectory of your life. Trust that, even if the exact vision isn't met, you'll gain wisdom. Even small changes can have a big impact over time.

Did you know? Inventing an excuse is a way to postpone taking action or to evade responsibility. Jon Taffer reminds us: "Excuses destroy success every time."

Regardless of how often you let up, find strength to continue and follow your desires. Live the life you wish for. A mantra to repel hesitation: *I won't miss out—an excuse isn't a solution.*

In a Nutshell

* Wear your body armor—be strong. Don't be deterred.

* Skip procrastinating: Value time; make yourself proud.

* Curb the next excuse; run interference—no cop-outs.

Things To Remember:

How we spend our free time is a choice. Why not make your days productive and enjoyable? Choose your path—align with your destiny. Make a pact and aim for what's heartfelt with perseverance. Design your life to reach the maximum potential. Shed insecurity and dismiss the negative voice from creeping in. Believe in yourself! Why impose limitations? Challenge yourself to make positive changes. Own your confidence; manage fear and excuses. Why hold back? Let the decisions become a compass directing toward your desired goals.

* Walk your path with consistency and determination.

* *Daily decisions determine destiny*—no box-checking.

* Replace fear with belief—make the pact; do the work.

* Rise to your potential; courageously lead the charge.

* Live confidently: Use *I believe in myself* as a mantra.

* Prevent self-sabotage; break out of your straitjacket.

* Make time: Push forward and pursue those big dreams.

* Reflect before trusting naysayers. Don't limit yourself.

* Highlight a positive view—thoughts impact outcomes.

* Curb excuses and procrastination; quit a vicious cycle.

Thoughts:

Motivational Checklist: Visit thedailydecisions.com/inspire

You're the one person who can change your life.

Anecdote:

Here's a life lesson I learned: Think before you react, rather than letting anger gain control.

Caught up in the drama of the moment—getting heated during a work phone call was the reason I almost lost my job. After the fact, defending myself and my value was thoroughly upsetting.

Time to look inward and reflect. Disappointment in my conduct led to this decision—to practice self-control and work on not lashing out again.

Step 2: Ditch Bad Habits

It's a big decision to change the direction of our lives. Taking stock and reconciling with both good and bad habits can be life-altering. Make the agreement! Why hold on to anything destructive?

Replacing negative behaviors with positive ones and removing barriers are choices that offer lasting benefits, allowing for forward movement.

Key Takeaway:

Rage leaves damage in its wake and isn't a good solution. The repercussions taught me that patience and kindness lead to better outcomes.

Work to break free from negativity and toxic patterns, such as impatience, anger, or rash responses that impede positive results. Examine the situation before reacting, and be tolerant.

Think first, take pause, and then take action. Don't underestimate the effect of a pleasant word.

Release The Toxic

Thinking positively and managing negativity
pave the way to more gratifying returns.

The Commitment

Take inventory of both positive and negative behaviors. Live aware! Bid farewell to the toxic people, thoughts, and actions that disrupt your life. Every time something counterproductive rears its ugly head, squash it before it festers and ruins another day.

Do you find that harmful behaviors tend to cycle repeatedly? Created over time, they may continue, even when intuition cautions that they're detrimental.

Bad habits might feel like old friends. In reality, toxic relationships, addictions, and defeatist thoughts are unhealthy and cause distress. The good news is change is our decision.

Before going down the rabbit hole, ask yourself the million-dollar question: Why allow your damaging behavior to persist? Learn to heed the warning signs and take charge.

1. *A helpful approach*: Pay attention to what triggers unsettling thoughts. Get tough and cut ties with those who manipulate or try to control you. Professional advice can also be helpful.

2. *Reflection*: Why catastrophize and jump to the worst possible conclusion after a minor setback? Instead: 1. Keep thoughts in check. 2. Test if there's proof. 3. Always add self-respect.

3. *Consider this:* Although the familiar may be welcoming, if it's harmful, safely dump it. Release the contaminants—the devious people, toxic behaviors, and destructive actions.

 *Start Now:* **FLIP THE SCRIPT!**

Try a fear or dread litmus test. Trace through your normal routine and notice things that give you an uneasy gut feeling. Ask yourself: Is the source fear of the next challenge, or dread over something toxic?

When facing harmful situations, take a pause and move in a direction that best offers perspective. Why make things difficult? Care for yourself—choose practical over emotional.

Picture this: There have been times in my life when I allowed people to influence my self-view. Sound familiar? While working as a designer, a competitive (possibly jealous) colleague told co-workers I lacked talent. It shook my confidence. Deciding not to get defensive, I let my work prove my worth. The lesson: Don't permit the actions of others to break your spirit—consider their intentions. A tip: Building self-trust helps resolve insecurities.

Positivity and confidence can free our minds from malignant thoughts and are keys to leading a self-nurturing lifestyle.

When confronted with cruel people or pessimistic views, my mantra is: *Unkind words, internal or external—denied entry.*

In a Nutshell

* Diligently release the negative and tenderly self-nurture.

* When you know it's bad for you—run; steer clear of it.

* Discard the toxic: Stop banging your head—move on.

Quiet Your Mind's Chatter

Take charge of thoughts, emotions, and behaviors.
Don't let them control you. Own your journey.

————————————

The Commitment

Make a conscious effort to quiet your mind's chatter so it doesn't get the best of you. Manage non-productive thoughts. Consider this: Why should I unfairly criticize myself and allow a negative perspective to impact my well-being? Develop a strategy for a rewarding future.

————————————

Do you hear your mind talk, talk, talking? Does it get you riled up? Is the jibber-jabber in your head negatively biased?

Did you know? Studies have shown that *negativity bias* is real. Our minds tend to remember negative information over positive. Embrace optimism—we can reshape our thinking.

Have you imagined all the bad things that could or might happen? Really, do they ever? My money's on *rarely*. Call to action: Think first and prevent the tizzy.

This realization led to my solution: Our thoughts are powerful. I stopped belittling myself and finding fault without cause. Whether in the mind or out loud: 1. Curb a critical voice. Say anything enough—it's what the brain believes. 2. Resist inner hostile chit-chat. 3. Self-kindness is soothing.

Never think of yourself as less than. How we see ourselves— whether as a winner or loser—shapes our actions and is evident to others. Practicing positive behaviors forms good habits.

When catching disruptive thoughts on loop, counter with fresh, positive dialogue. Add self-belief and speak only constructively about yourself. Then, notice an attitude shift.

 *Start Now*: **DITCH THE HABIT!**

End the negative conversation with a brand-new talk track. Think of a few replacement thoughts to keep on hand. For example, replace I messed up again or I'm so stupid with I love learning something new.

My secret weapon: Unclench your teeth and train your mind to repeat positive thoughts that resonate with personal goals.

I pushed one step further and thought about all the good in my life. Gratitude and appreciation help foster positivity and enhance the potential for achieving better results.

Another solution: Offer yourself some tender loving care. Strive to seek out the good, not what's lacking. This mindset helps quiet doubt and creates a more favorable impact.

Focusing on kindness can help put worry into perspective. Consider *Limbitless Solutions*, a nonprofit co-founded by Albert Manero, that provides 3D-printed prosthetics for those in need.

A mantra can be helpful and as simple as: *Think positively!* Reminder: Attitude is important.

In a Nutshell

* Train your mind; think about creating a positive impact.

* Make a conscious effort to end the negative talk track.

* Tune in: Work on monitoring thoughts and actions.

Manage Stress And Welcome Calm

Laughter is a mood booster that's free.

_____

The Commitment

The goal: Discourage what can't be controlled from becoming a source of stress. Worrying invites problems, depletes energy, and solves nothing. Avoiding these situations saves endless hours, yielding precious moments to enjoy.

_____

Has feeling stressed become a pattern that developed over time? We can't control outside forces. We can learn to manage our emotions and actions. Pause and calm down.

Life isn't always peachy and some days might feel like the pits. How we behave, think, and act is a choice.

Imagine the day is going well when suddenly your phone rings, and a co-worker or family member makes a derogatory comment, finding fault with you. The stress starts to creep into this perfectly fine day. That's a yellow light. Strategy review:

1. Slow yourself down. Take time to breathe. Permit positive energy only. Recall your good qualities. Life will go on. The objective: Enjoy the day. Run from hissy fits and keep calm.

2. Be gentle with yourself; make a decision to keep joy alive.

3. Choose to self-soothe. Reflect, organize, take a break, walk, journal, manage what happens next, and remove regret.

Have you witnessed how destructive a stress meltdown feels to all involved, during and after? Think before reacting.

$Start$ Now: CHANGE THINGS UP!

Research indicates that in stressful moments, physically smiling can trigger feelings of happiness. Additionally, laughter boosts mood, releases tension, relaxes the mind and body, decreases cortisol (the stress hormone), and increases endorphins.

Whether long-term or short-term, unchecked strain can cause damage. One person's tension is different from someone else's. Learning to manage our stressors and maintaining balance helps us achieve well-being.

Does stress agitate your temper or escalate irritability? Do you worry when facing something new or unexpected? Stay aware of the triggers. Fight to stay in control. Recognize what you sense. I feel pressure in my head and churning in my gut.

Do you feel out of sorts after losing your composure, no longer able to think rationally? That's no fun. How we react will let us handle the situation or give our emotions the upper hand.

Commission your creativity. My go-to stress reducers: Music, art, exercise, and dancing. Find yours! Practice this mantra: *I choose a calm mind.* Woo joy, not angst; ease overwhelm.

In a Nutshell

* Practice taming stressors daily. Talk it out; build a habit.

* Manage stressful moments; don't let them control you.

* Stay aware of the triggers. Seek professional advice.

Fear Limits Outcome And Perfection Prevents Progress

Your past challenges don't define you; they are stepping stones for growth.

The Commitment

Make a pledge! Accept yourself, ease up, and add some slack. Do your best, and try not to be so hard on yourself. Learn from the past and move forward. Perfection is more of an ideal than a reality. We all make mistakes. Fear is normal, but not sustainable.

Does perfection have you stuck, afraid of not measuring up, and unable to make decisions? Unburden yourself; remove the words *failure* and *perfect*. Embrace the unknown, and while you're at it, give some love to the imperfectly perfect you.

The world may feel as though it adores perfection, with retouched images revered and put on pedestals. Instead of buying in, invest in these words: *I am enough.*

Picture this: Well-known actress Emily Blunt struggled with a stuttering problem during her youth. While in secondary school, a teacher encouraged her to try out for a play by using accents and character voices when speaking the words. She overcame her stutter and found confidence. Find your strategy!

Reality check: Perfection has been my battle. I calculated success by my perception of others. I finally reconciled with Shakespeare's view: "All that glitters is not gold."

Think about this: Perfection often isn't what it seems. Beneath the surface lurks the truth. How did I shift? I memorialized the occasion with a letter, managed fear, and accepted myself.

Dear perfection: We're through! Breaking up is hard, but I'm tough. Good riddance to bad habits that halt progress. Bye-bye time-wasting, excuses, overanalyzing, and low esteem.

 *Start Now*: **TAKE THE LEAP!**

> ***Work to calm overwhelm***: **Write down five fears that prevent you from striving for growth. For each, note a positive counter-thought and motivation booster.**

Fear can be a limiting emotion, a hardwired mechanism our brains use to protect us from danger. When in peril, run. If not, face facts, release doubt, and use time effectively.

Break the cycle: Push through and conquer your fear. Visions of failure, feelings of inadequacy, and judgment—self and external—can get in the way of pursuing the best possible life.

No, self-blocking: The desire to begin a project gets harder the more it's postponed, as rationalizations obstruct the way.

A mantra to have and to hold: *I am imperfectly perfect and accept myself. I am not my fears.*

In a Nutshell

* Step up: Take a chance and don't let fear limit the way.

* Perfection isn't reality—embrace your imperfections.

* Create a strategy: Why worry about what *might* be?

Lean Into Your Intuition

When things go wrong, pause and take a breath.
Learn to get out of your way.

The Commitment

Take care of the things within your control and do your best with everything else. Know when to trust your gut, clear the way, let it be, and give it up to the universe. Avoid a surefire time zap.

Have you noticed when you try too hard, or overdo something, the result may not be ideal? Do you hear a little voice or see a mental picture (your intuition cautioning) and ignore it?

When something goes wrong, do you find yourself feeling letdown? Do you ever think, if only I'd paid attention to my intuition? Remember, when the inner alarm goes off, observe and tune into that small, strong call. Examine your premonition!

Help is here—take notice. Intuition is accessible to all. Once your awareness is attuned, it becomes easier to recognize and adjust before any challenges occur.

Keying into that inner voice (your guide), while respecting the red flags, alleviates subsequent problems and frustration from arising. Use it as a pivot point to avoid any remorse. From now on, dial in, think twice, and proceed with foresight.

My guiding mantra: *Lean on instincts—preserve well-being.*

Trust experience: When you feel the signal to stop, listen. Or, perhaps your sixth sense is urging you to go forward and do something else. Consider saying yes!

Picture this: While working in sales, I learned a valuable lesson when my gut advised me to take a customer off my call list. Not listening and going anyhow proved my internal partner correct. The upshot: The customer became argumentative after asking for information that wasn't available. My conclusion is that we can't always win people over. Why make it personal? Rely on those inner feelings—they can reveal the best direction to take.

 *Start Now*: **FLIP THE SCRIPT!**

Use the statement: I've got this—I have a trusted advisor. Remember: *Your* intuition is *your* secret inner guide. Try it out, note if it worked, record, or mentally jot any lessons learned.

Self-care: Research suggests intuitive decisions stem from data accumulated through past experiences. By recognizing patterns, our brains release neurochemicals that guide our thought processes. Stay mindful and prioritize your well-being.

Check in: Allow self-trust to breathe through. Reflect before acting, and tune into your inner ally. You've got this! Good news: Intuition can get more refined with use. Learn, adapt, grow!

In a Nutshell

* Sharpen awareness by incorporating intuition journaling.

* Aha, align with your inner guide and steer your course.

* Tune in to avoid problems before they take hold.

Don't Let Others Define You

Reshape unproductive thoughts. Own your priorities. Replace what isn't working with empowering choices.

_____

The Commitment

Resist the manipulative people, who enjoy making others feel inferior by dictating how to live and what to think. Claim the power to challenge their verdict and then high-five your decision.

_____

Do you know anyone who tries to make others feel second-rate, dragging them down and causing trouble for incomprehensible reasons to stroke their ego? If so, repeat these words with a smile: I'll define myself, thank you very much.

Think about it: Spiteful people might wreak havoc at someone else's expense to boost their mood and confidence. Logically speaking, causes can vary—ranging from misunderstandings and jealousy to the need to justify a job or a desire to fit in.

Advice to self: Be aware when gossip sneaks into conversations. Retreat and don't engage. Other people's opinions are *theirs*—make up your *own* mind.

> Picture this: Chris Gardner's inspirational story portrayed in *The Pursuit of Happyness* inspires self-belief. While homeless, he raised a son and put in the effort to improve his life. Gardner became a stockbroker and started a brokerage firm. The lesson is to persist, unleash your superpowers, and define yourself.

Why let negative thoughts cloud your mind, as they can lead to feelings of upset and inadequacy? Instead, own your value. Just as you shouldn't judge a book by its cover, don't base your self-worth on idle chatter.

So many people follow the herd rather than trailblaze. Trust yourself, be brave, honor your beliefs, and remain flexible. Reminder—perspective cautions: In a world of billions, why allow a few to determine *your* destiny? Make it *your* choice.

 *Start Now*: **DITCH THE HABIT!**

If you find yourself believing anyone else's version of you, challenge that thinking. If it's *true*, write down *your* takeaway, and try expressing the insight you gained. If it's *false*, document the real story, and then practice verbalizing *your* truth.

Make a promise: Paint your picture and report your own news. Why give another individual that control? The solution: Nurture self-belief to help face challenges with confidence and adaptability. Let's toast to that!

Ensure *you're* the ruling authority in *your* life's vision. Why allow anyone the ability to undermine *your* qualifications? Instead, stay positive, embody conviction, and react to what feels right. Rinse and repeat this mantra: *I believe in myself!*

In a Nutshell

* Make a binding decision: Don't be defined by others.

* Question anyone who tries to shake your confidence.

* Recognize gossip: Trust yourself wholeheartedly.

Conquer Your Inner Bully

Never forget to respect and protect yourself.

_____

The Commitment

Have faith in your potential. Address counterproductive thoughts. Avoid putting yourself down. Acknowledge your abilities and create who you become. Thoughts play an important part in the results. Find that SPF—your self-protection factor.

_____

Is your energy zapped from obsessing ad nauseam over everything you said or did, even though it's impossible to undo what occurred in the past? Cut the circuit on that habit.

These types of self-induced thoughts have been referred to as the *inner bully*. If this has become a comfortable act, realize how destructive it is. Accept that you deserve better. Fight back! My truce: Block the noise and end self-criticism.

1. *Ask yourself*: Will circular thinking, dwelling on could haves, feeling you don't measure up, and taunting yourself help?

2. In reaction to threats, *fight or flight* responses are triggered by fear. Recognizing these feelings in the moment helps to stay aware and remain in control. It's a useful strategy.

3. Why not be satisfied by doing the best *you* can? Work on adjusting *your* thought process. A mantra to the rescue: *I love myself. I'm capable!* Now move on and enjoy this moment.

4. Why waste energy being your own enemy? Instead, become your champion. Embrace life and seize the opportunities.

 *Start Now*: **CHANGE THINGS UP!**

> **As a warmup, take twenty minutes in your day to consider someone you know who has been bullied. Write down three kind things about that person and write a few nice words describing yourself.**

Key aim: Make peace with your inner critic. Change the conversation with that decision and advocate for yourself, to yourself. Promise to train your mind to be personally considerate.

It's important to address bullying to prevent emotional damage and ensure safety, and it is equally necessary to set ground rules that halt self-bullying. Stay firm and confident in your worth. Finally, make sure not to become a bully, even when feeling vulnerable. Compassion is crucial; we all deserve kindness.

Solution-time: 1. Permission to forgive—no one's perfect. 2. Distinguish truth from fiction. 3. Self-validation helps protect against insecurities. 4. Accept and learn from mistakes. Trading self-doubt for acceptance was my breakthrough.

No one's a *Superman* or *Superwoman*; instead, be your own hero. A cheerful disposition can save the day.

In a Nutshell

* Tame both inner and outer bullies. Uplift, don't damage.

* Superhumans are fictional—fight to be your own hero.

* Believe in yourself and shine both inside and out.

Control The Worry And Enjoy

Measure life by what truly matters.

_____

The Commitment

Why waste time worrying what others think, what might happen, or could be? Kick anguish, panic, and drama to the curb. Sing a mantra: Worry, self-doubt, and fear are no longer welcomed here.

_____

If you want to achieve your purpose and live a happier life, why let every little thing get in the way of that goal?

Message to self: Reason cautions, worrying gains nothing. Accept that not everything happens as expected, or turns out as planned. Some things are simply out of our hands.

Do you often find fault with yourself? My test proved to me a positive mindset contributes to better outcomes. Reassess, then prioritize nurturing kindness toward yourself each day.

Take a lesson from the past: There's no time like the present to send unproductive and illogical worry on its way.

> Picture this: Worry and fear plagued me until one evening, while out with friends, I realized that I'd forgotten to do something for a customer. Instead of fretting, I decided to try out some advice from entrepreneur Barbara Corcoran. I quickly thought about shifting my thoughts. Giving myself permission to handle it tomorrow freed my mind to enjoy. Having fun and truly being present was a lesson in not sweating the small stuff.

1. Avoid letting *coulda, shoulda* dominate your mind, and remind yourself that *hindsight is 20/20*. Letting go (not to be confused with giving up) is far healthier than holding on to what might have been. Learn from it and move on.

2. Constant dread is unsustainable—counter the torment, control the impulse, and cut the cord. Act instantly and fight to release that uncomfortable feeling.

 *Start Now*: **TAKE THE LEAP!**

> **When worry begins, focus on something else, such as exercise, work, music, meditation, or your breath. Shift away, distract, change direction, and step into a better mood with any constructive action that will charge up favorable energy.**

Think about this: Many daily concerns don't happen. Shape and refine the inner and outer view; recognize and manage unreasonable thoughts. Rein in the excessive worry cycle so that it no longer clouds your judgment and ruins the day.

A golden approach: Exit your comfort zone. Switch your attention and focus on productive tasks. Don't self-compromise. You deserve respect. Leave the grief—take the serenity.

Why not choose to adjust your mindset and calm self-doubt? It's doable with desire and practice. Live optimally!

In a Nutshell

* Kick worry to the curb; cut the cord—mindset matters.

* Ban coulda, shoulda, woulda—worrying solves nothing.

* Shift your thoughts—constant dread is unsustainable.

Things To Remember:

Take charge! Break up with those bad habits. Ask, who's the boss? Release the toxic. Quiet your mind's unfavorable chatter. Stand firm and don't put yourself down. Choose positivity over negativity—it's a shield from self-harm. Manage stress, worry, and fear, and welcome calm. Life should be your party, guest list included. Tune into intuition—it can be a useful guide. Ensure no one defines you; own the right. From today onward, stop putting off dreams and goals. Think of these reminders when you need them; be your own hero.

* Part ways with toxic behaviors, people, and situations.

* Cut the cord: Curb your mind's non-productive chatter.

* Choose to manage stress and welcome in the serenity.

* Nix living in fear: Why aim for perfection? Add self-love.

* Use your instincts and intuition. Scrutinize with caution.

* Own your priorities; don't let anyone set them for you.

* Engage the fire within and decide not to be defined.

* Live in truth; ensure that your life's direction feels right.

* Be personally considerate. Never self-bully or act rude.

* Replace worry: Switch to constructive activity—enjoy.

Thoughts:

_____

_____

_____

_____

_____

_____

_____

_____

_____

_____

_____

_____

_____

_____

_____

_____

_____

_____

_____

_____

_____

Happiness Worksheet: Visit thedailydecisions.com/inspire

A fulfilling life can't thrive with a pessimistic mindset.

Anecdote:

Perspective has proven to me that mindset plays a role in the will to secure and sustain a productive end result.

During the pattern design chapter of my career, I had a runaway hit—a leaf and texture combination in beautiful jewel-like colors. I always believed it would sell well. My confidence fueled the journey to see it through.

Many of the companies I licensed to reluctantly agreed, saying, "Well, maybe. Do you really think this is good?" My positive approach was integral; without it, their uncertainty would've been an excuse for them not to move forward. My belief drove their decisions to invest in and manufacture the product.

Step 3: The Mindset

Focus on what you can control. Adopting a proactive mindset rather than a reactive one can be empowering. Steer toward more desirable outcomes. Rally your courage and summon up a winning mentality—both are more likely to yield better results.

Walk the road of faith. Trust in your abilities, and ensure your conviction is conveyed to the world around you. As you shine your light, let it illuminate your path.

Key Takeaway:

Realize that what you share has value. Find power in thinking positively—it's a first-rate partner when working through life's problems.

Unhealthy ideas percolating in our minds can spoil a day. Take the reins and live self-aware.

One's outlook can become an ally when trained to be self-assured and optimistic, not pessimistic.

Develop a constructive mindset. Allow your thoughts to align with objectives, not distractions. Cultivate a calm mind and trust that it can lead to inner peace. Enjoy more and worry less.

Dream It – Live It

Embrace the courage to pursue your dreams
and work toward making them a reality.

_____

The Commitment

*Include: Self-belief and a leap of faith. Hold a picture of your future
close to your heart, and proceed with passion. Reaching for your
goals is a way to confirm what's possible.*

_____

Do you dream about that next accomplishment? Whether it's
big and life-altering, or a small next step, now's the time to
start. My mantra: *Action and grit yield the reward.*

Once you envision an idea, will you respond and move forward? A positive mindset lays the foundation for success.

I understand from my own struggles that many things get in
the way of pursuing and fulfilling our dreams. Only we can
make space to explore and complete what matters to us.

Self-reflection: Purpose encouraged my decision to make a
change. The deciding factor was, drumroll, please: Let nothing block me from going after anything that's truly heartfelt.

Satisfying my deepest desires was integral to living fully.
When dreams linger, lift the curtain, and give them the stage.

Mindset matters! Step back from people that zap your spirit.

Start Now: **TAKE THE LEAP!**

What can you do if you feel unmotivated? Consider using reverse psychology to reignite your passion. Say aloud: I'm not willing to hit my goals. Then let the dissonance of that statement serve as motivation to address what's really holding you back. Push through and move forward.

What keeps tugging at your heart? Simply ask yourself: Why not go after it? So much is viable with devotion and discipline. Wishing isn't enough; work is vital. Visualize hitting your target. Take the challenge and follow through.

Personal musings: I often wonder about those who achieved greatness, revolutionized the world, led through rough times, developed new technologies, or entertained us. No path is easy. Focus, determination, and resilience are keys to success.

Picture this: The actress Hedy Lamarr, popular in the 1940s, used her breaks between scenes to work on inventions, one of which was called frequency hopping—the technology that paved the way for today's Wi-Fi, Bluetooth, and GPS. Live inspired! Why not make your ideas a reality?

Remind yourself: Taking charge of your schedule enhances productivity. Getting into motion can help end self-pity, improve time management, and inspire perseverance. There's no telling what's possible. Effort opens doors.

In a Nutshell

* Release doubt: Approach every day with appreciation.

* Commit, then make time to strive toward your dream.

* Work to achieve whatever it is that's summoning you.

Believe And Stay Positive

An uplifting thought each morning
can brighten the day ahead.

The Commitment

Mirror the change you want to see. Instead of being hesitant, draw on your positivity and skills. Depend on yourself for validation—no one else. Please, stop feeling sorry for yourself; it's not productive.

The objective: Make today's intention to stay the course and follow through on one goal. Persevere, head in an upward direction, and guard against harmful thoughts. Aspire to live with confidence—allow it to shine through.

Why do some people live at the address of *I can't*? While taking a social media class, I listened to other students who were ready to give up without even trying.

Reflect on the damage of burying a life's desire with a mindset like: Why bother if I'm not going to make it big? We all begin at square one—true success often takes years of hard work.

Question to yourself: What if you took the time to master what you're working on and enjoy the journey?

Remain hopeful and optimistic! Consider tuning out those who preach that it's not possible. Both positivity and negativity are contagious. Each is a choice to champion and spread.

 *Start Now*: **CHANGE THINGS UP!**

Reminder: Use portion control to prevent big goal burnout. Break it down so it's manageable. Focus your mind and be clear on each task to override procrastination. Start by blocking time on your daily calendar. Set an alert and take these appointments seriously. Track and celebrate progress to stimulate momentum.

My realization: Adding encouragement to keep going can help avoid stress and excuses that obstruct reaching the finish line. Purpose is the motivator; passion adds the energy.

Think about this: Accomplishment is exciting and offers hope for the future, as demonstrated by Reshma Saujani, who recognized a need to close the gender gap in the technology industry. Determined, she started the nonprofit, *Girls Who Code*. It's now available in all fifty states and has helped young women decide to pursue computer science in college.

Examine this idea: Create a *positive* self-fulfilling prophecy. Expectations influence behavior. Confidence can bring newfound enthusiasm, while it's absence may close off options.

My commitment: Be mindful before giving in to doubt. Move forward. Step into this mantra: *Positive over negative; fuel self-belief.* Unleash your dedication and spunk. Join me!

In a Nutshell

* Feed your positive energy; resist the negative. Share it.

* Nurture your ambitions and banish the words, *I can't*.

* Believe in yourself and the value you bring. Master it.

Think Happy Thoughts
Happiness Is A Choice

Money and material things bring temporary happiness; capturing joy and personal fulfillment is the prize.

The Commitment

When a discouraging thought arises, counter it with a reassuring one. Stand up to people who try to steal your happiness and put a damper on the day. Fight to protect your well-being. Hold on to joy!

Some days are tough to get through, burdened by unease and emotional tumult, which amplifies vulnerability. *Why be a victim?* Instead, accept the situation and channel self-kindness.

Reinforce: It's important to recognize that excessive self-blame is harmful and hinders progress. Focus on your strengths.

Truth speaks: There are always things to improve upon. Gently and with a positive mindset, be honest and confront whatever troubling habits need a makeover. Toast change!

Memo: Happiness is a choice influenced by perspective. Resist the culprits—those lethal thoughts, devious individuals, and harmful situations. Take charge and find your supporters.

My ask: Why not celebrate what makes each of us special? Practice rewording derogatory self-talk to include compliments, gratitude, and congrats throughout the day.

Defeatism is an enemy to shake; confidence is the defense. My long overdue mantra: *Welcome a bright outlook; practice daily.*

 *Start Now*: **DITCH THE HABIT!**

Develop a gentleness when doubt or pessimistic talk eclipses your mind. Instead, take a moment to recollect a few happy thoughts. How? Think of a friend who loves you very much. Chat live to gain their perspective. Then, carve out time to write positively about yourself.

Shift: It's necessary to reevaluate the power given to those who deflate the wind from our sails. Try to avoid these situations, or limit contact, and if possible, simply disengage.

Self-promise: Embrace good energy and release the bad. Seek calm and choose optimism. Keep emotions in check. Now notice, many times what clouds the way is no longer important.

Big aha: Our decisions can often make or break the day. When conflicting thoughts arise, or unexpected events happen, the impact depends on how we respond.

Research suggests that laughter, gratitude, and acts of kindness can elevate serotonin and dopamine levels. Certain foods, such as leafy greens, salmon, berries, and nuts—along with others—may also boost mood by increasing these neurotransmitters.

In a Nutshell

* Invite the happiness to enter—make it a daily decision.

* Reevaluate those in your circle; find your joyful place.

* Adopt a cheerful disposition—foster inner peace.

Live Life On Your Terms

Don't be limited by anyone's expectations, be yourself.

———————

The Commitment

Be true to yourself. Why let anyone spoil one sliver of your day? Let's be clear: Make sure you live your life. Don't stand in someone else's shadow. Own the story. Take the lead—meet the challenge and reveal your true potential. You got me?

———————

Self-ownership: Take responsibility for your future. Why not make a promise to live on your terms? Commit to cultivating what lies ahead, instead of leaving it to chance.

Remaining true to your core values is helpful when crafting any plan—ensure joy's included. Stay alert! Watch for opportunities that best suit you to shine through. Place the bet on you.

A key focus: Don't let apathy set in, or allow someone else to decide your destiny. Why should other people's skepticism or cynicism interfere with living a fulfilling life? It's about the mindset—feed it with bravery, not fear.

Why do yourself a disservice and give up on something that's important to you each time someone disapproves? Big dreams aren't temporary; they live within us, starving to be nourished. Instead of putting the brakes on progress, draw from inner strength. Channel Oliver Twist: "Please sir, I want some more." Now, fill 'er up.

Lessons to initiate balance: 1. Put energy into creating new accomplishments, not into unsettling thoughts. 2. Maintain an honest perspective. 3. Make each day meaningful.

Start Now: **FLIP THE SCRIPT!**

When criticism's ringing in your ears, think of dislodging the song that's stuck repeating, over and over. Click a different station; change the tune with some lively music and happy lyrics. Physically step into the new sound.

When doubt enters my mind, it helps to ask earnestly: Why should I choose to lose out on the life I deserve to live?

> Picture this: Told he had no imagination, Walt Disney was fired from his first job at a newspaper. He then created an animation company that went bankrupt and kept trying until he succeeded. Over three hundred banks and investors rejected his theme park vision. Not deterred by setbacks, Walt built the *Disney* dream. Lucky for us, he didn't lose sight of his mission. Make your magic!

My belief: Work steadily toward each day's objectives. Most aspirations don't occur overnight and certainly won't happen without taking a crack at it. So, why stagnate, or stifle your inner cravings?

The path will twist and turn. Instead of succumbing to obstacles or indecision, awaken your inner navigator. Live life on your terms. Think Frank Sinatra—own this mantra: *"I did it my way!"*

In a Nutshell

* Aim to keep calm and don't put the brakes on progress.

* Walk the path on your terms: Be willing to twist and turn.

* Go the distance: Take responsibility for your self-growth.

Don't Give In To Intimidation

It's important to remember: No one's perfect; becoming your best self is the reward.

_____

The Commitment

Trust your principles and seek strength from within, even when faced with intimidation, skepticism, and pressure. It's okay to stand your ground. Embrace your values and let them guide you. Believe in yourself and remain authentic. Infuse your efforts with heart, a resilient mindset, and positivity.

_____

Say yes to being receptive. Listen with an open mind when sensible advice and insights are offered. Dial in and be discerning when people suggest doing things in *their* best interest, not *yours*. Take time to differentiate between the two.

Be bold: Why try to fit in when you can stand out? Make a plan, create a schedule, and resist getting trapped in someone else's skepticism. 1. Own your value. 2. Lean into your intuition when it signals. 3. Answer to yourself honestly.

Self-truth: Why be a people pleaser to gain acceptance? Offer help for the right reasons, not due to intimidation. My change in perspective: Not allowing myself to be controlled by what others think helps alleviate feelings of uncertainty.

Huge aha: Give yourself credit and resist succumbing to pressure. As I've learned, don't be afraid to say: *No, this is my life!*

A mantra to ignite today: *It's my choice; I'll decide for myself.*

Assignment: 1. Follow your heart. 2. Always hold self-worth in high regard. 3. Don't sell yourself short.

 *Start Now*: **CHANGE THINGS UP!**

Visualize this: You have a terrific idea, but someone is planting doubt. Use the Lazy Susan technique and turn the tables. Adopt the code phrase: Thanks, I appreciate your input to stop the flow of unwanted advice and negative vibes. Now, smile!

Call to action: Why live afraid? Take a chance. Either stay in the same place or act on your dreams. Sharpen new skills, spotlight them, and highlight your achieved mastery.

Pinterest co-founder Ben Silbermann wasn't deterred when his startup didn't achieve overnight success. Rather than giving in to skepticism, he left his full-time job to focus on building the company. Now worth billions of dollars, it's a lesson in self-belief. Stay true to yourself.

Think about this: Calmly standing up for yourself is not rude or aggressive—it reflects confidence and is a validation of your worth. Release shame and embarrassment. Instead, trust, love, and accept yourself—it's then you can thrive.

It's our mindset that can propel us forward or hold us back. Stop building barriers. Consistent effort often triumphs in the end. Make one of the daily decisions to nurture your well-being.

In a Nutshell

* Remain true to yourself: Don't be ashamed; be proud.

* Push through intimidation; put value on your worth.

* Follow the leader—it's you. Craft an enjoyable life.

Walk Away From Negativity

Trade negative thoughts for positive ones.
Open the door and invite five-star results to enter.

———————

The Commitment

Resist negativity—it can compromise positive results. Pursue your purpose. Defend yourself against anything or anyone that limits forward momentum en route to living your best life.

———————

Are you caught up in a plague of pessimism, conceding to unflattering thoughts, or accepting demeaning comments that destroy your morale? 1. If so, ask why? 2. Shift your mindset. 3. Work on creating new positive patterns.

Reminder: The brain, dating back to early humans, tends to prioritize negative information over positive. The good news is we can reframe our thoughts and reshape our perspective.

Negative behaviors are self-defeating. They may disrupt our plans or cause us to give up and crush our expectations. Recognizing and understanding this can help us to change. Face it—it's a choice! Why not make it a rule to think positively?

Self-agreement: I'll no longer dedicate time to criticism without proof. Noticing that internal or external degrading chatter isn't always based on truth, I dismiss it from claiming my attention.

Live joyfully: 1. Resist anything or anyone that distracts from living with a positive view. 2. Magnify kindness and mute hate.

Picture this: Oprah Winfrey is widely recognized as an inspirational and charismatic icon. Having endured abuse at a young age, her journey wasn't easy. Winfrey was a news anchor, hosted a successful talk show, launched a magazine, and created a TV network, while generously giving back. Even with newsworthy setbacks, criticism, and negativity, she's never given up. Her trusted words serve as motivation for many. Her impact is felt throughout the world.

There's no escaping haters. I pledged to stop placating them, replacing toxic influencers with open-minded supporters who care. Choose wisely, as this can impact the course of your life.

 *Start Now*: **DITCH THE HABIT!**

Walk it off! Get literal about walking away. Trek along a favorite path for twenty minutes. Set the intention: With every stride taken, a little piece of negativity is left behind. For fun, consult a step tracker. Research suggests that walking releases endorphins, boosts mood, and can decrease sensitivity to stress and pain.

Check in: Set the pace. A healthy perspective lights the way. Manage your thinking and direct your progress. Take that big step and keep on heading toward your destination.

Self-love is due: Recognize the poisonous inner critic when it comes to visit. Throw away the welcome mat—bolt the door. Repeating the cycle and not moving forward is a self-imposed limitation. A mantra for a mindset change: *I will resist negativity.*

In a Nutshell

* Initiate progress: Manage that non-productive outlook.

* Reframe your mindset; ban what detracts and distracts.

* Replace each negative thought with a positive choice.

You Are Who You Think You Are

Believe in yourself. Add a positive mindset.
Climb your mountain with courage.

_____

The Commitment

Believe that you are worthy. Trust that your strength lies within. Cultivate self-esteem. Share that attitude with others and inspire the respect you deserve.

_____

Do you ever feel that you don't measure up? Appearances can be deceiving. "The grass isn't always greener on the other side."

Think about this: Spotlight your good qualities—lean into self-belief. Learn, grow, and train your mind not to focus on the negative. Feed hope!

Unlock self-confidence: Why assume that others have more to contribute? Trust in this message: We all have our own gifts. Remember—you are who you think you are.

The truth: Feeling worthless is counterproductive. Self-image is expressed in our demeanor and spreads externally. Emotions within are transferred outward. Emerge unstoppable!

The decision to grow into our best selves takes effort. The lessons I learned validated that positivity wins. Approaching any situation with conviction can help create trust. It's beneficial to keep that thought in mind. Have faith in yourself.

Invite this liberating mantra in daily: *I believe in my value; it can't be erased.* Live confidently and be true to *your* path.

Picture this: Well-known author and illustrator Jeff Kinney demonstrates that pivoting and adapting are keys to success. While attending the University of Maryland, Kinney created a popular comic strip for its newspaper, inspiring his goal to become a syndicated cartoonist.

When that didn't happen, he started writing *Diary of a Wimpy Kid*. A while later, a website posted it in daily installments. Next, a book publisher chose to publish it for kids. Although Kinney first believed his fans were adults, he agreed. My takeaway: Do what you love, with trust, flexibility, and belief—let it lead you to where you are meant to be.

 *Start Now*: **FLIP THE SCRIPT!**

Use the running list method. Keep a journal with you. Every time you have a moment of self-doubt, counter it with a positive skill set and accomplishment. Write them down, review each evening, and practice self-love.

Every person's journey is shaped by their desires. When feeling apprehensive, ask: Why compare myself to others? Embrace your abilities and shine brightly!

Tap into inner strength. Unleash self-worth. Then, muster up the will to honor yourself, and defend your dignity.

In a Nutshell

* Radiate self-belief and boldly share your gifts outward.

* Keep thoughts in check: Add courage; own your value.

* Think it to become it—nurture confidence in yourself.

Be Kind To Yourself

What makes you different is what makes you, *you*.

The Commitment

Strive to do your best and rise to a challenge. On the flip side, be understanding, shower kindness, and self-respect when things don't work to plan. Try again tomorrow.

Now and then it's better to take a break and rejuvenate, rather than push yourself to exhaustion. Why not take a pause? It might be exactly what's needed to restore *your* energy.

I attest: Anyone can fall victim to the rote habit of running themselves ragged. Refreshingly, this exact pattern is one of the most enjoyable to quit. Nevertheless, avoid using a break as the excuse to give up on that goal, or life adventure.

Make today count: Many of us have little choice except to work for a living, which may lack gratification. Ease up and be gentle. Why be so hard on yourself? Step-by-step, reach for *your* heartfelt desires.

Lights on: Be kind to one-and-only *you*. There's something to be said for doing things that nourish satisfaction and inner peace. It's easier to start and finish anything with that view.

Don't put off self-care: Be honest; know when to rest. Love yourself enough to recharge and reclaim *you-time*.

Greet well-being: Staying healthy in mind and spirit is a helpful part of living an accomplished and content life.

 *Start Now*: **TAKE THE LEAP!**

Personal care: Remember a blissful time. Think of a peaceful environment. Find a quote or keepsake that helps to easily recall the memory. Keep it with you and use it to soothe your mind in moments of tension.

Self-talk: Red light the flow of hurtful words. Why feel pushed until there's nothing left to give? Green light treating yourself with dignity. Unlock your mind and let the sun shine in.

> Picture this: I was falling behind, not pleased with the pace of my day. My *inner bully* ran wild calling me cruel names. At that moment, I took charge of my narrative, recognized the internal dialogue for what it was, silenced that inner voice from wreaking havoc, and embraced more realistic expectations. Your turn!

Come to terms with this message: I'm doing the best I can. While pursuing goals, it's important to award yourself some grace and applause. This action invites enjoyment into the process. Aha, creating peace of mind helps to flourish.

A mantra to hug: *I will be kind inward and outward every day.* Self-tenderness and welcoming joy are contributors to quality of life. Personal fulfillment nourishes productivity.

In a Nutshell

* Know when to take a break: Reclaim energy—replenish!

* Seek contentment, satisfy the soul, and greet pleasure.

* Treat yourself with kindness and respect, not abuse.

Things To Remember:

Appreciate yourself. Make time to go after and achieve your dreams. Stay positive—break free from pessimistic paralysis. Embrace this as a daily decision: Own your value. Self-belief helps build trust. Cultivate the challenge to live life your way. Resist giving in to intimidation and walk away from negativity. Be kind to yourself. Release doubt, add courage, and reclaim energy. Don't bury your ambitions. Achieve whatever it is that's summoning you. Tap into inner peace. Reminder: You are who you think you are. Incorporate this mindset daily.

* Trust yourself: Defy skepticism and follow your heart.

* Own self-belief; keep positivity in check. Say: *Yes, I can.*

* Let the joy in; make happiness the overriding decision.

* Manage life on your terms; be the leader—nix conflict.

* Nurture self-worth; keep it top of mind. Enjoy this life.

* Reframe your mindset; ban what detracts and distracts.

* Choose to replace negative choices with positive ones.

* Liberate: Don't permit others to dictate your thoughts.

* Self-memo: The internal message is projected outward.

* Self-kindness fosters a healthy mind, spirit, and respect.

Thoughts:

_____

_____

_____

_____

_____

_____

_____

_____

_____

_____

_____

_____

_____

_____

_____

_____

_____

_____

_____

_____

_____

_____

Feel-Good Activity List: Visit thedailydecisions.com/inspire

Believing is a key to achieving. Don't be afraid to be great.

Anecdote:

One of my favorite ways to start any project is to make a written step-by-step plan. That was my approach when writing this book. I outlined each topic and included solutions to change habits that kept me from living fulfilled and in balance. My goal is that my strategies help you, too.

This guidebook evolved from the suggestion that my personal challenges are common, and that sharing my remedies for each improvement I made might help others live happier lives.

Over time, it was harder not to take initiative. I committed to my goals, moved forward, and celebrated the wins. These efforts made facing obstacles more gratifying.

Step 4: The Action

We all have yearnings. It's worthwhile to value and pursue what truly matters. Otherwise, a part of us is lost, and sadly, we will never know what could've been.

Take charge and use energy wisely. Set aside time to work on what's important to you. Keep the faith. Let nothing break your spirit. On the count of three—starting now—rolling and action!

Key Takeaway:

Anything worth achieving rarely happens on its own. As mentioned, positivity, self-belief, calm reflection, and flexibility are helpful for growth. Manage fear and take responsibility. Find your supporters and ask for a push when the next excuse surfaces.

Live determined! Why not take this challenge and live life with drive? Discover your passion, give it the green light, and jump-start your activity.

It's natural to feel afraid. Why let uncertainty or procrastination get in the way of arriving at your personal best? It's within each of us to change by agreeing to conquer what stops us.

Motivate Yourself Every Day

To ensure productivity, add a firm deadline.

The Commitment

When in doubt, ask: Why give up? Then, agree to take action and satisfy the hunger within. Architect a strategic plan and follow it through. Wishing and hoping won't cut it. Forward motion is the difference between reading the pages and completing the book, or never knowing the outcome. Choose to start and finish.

On occasion, do you think about a personal aspiration, then put it on the back burner in favor of the distraction at the moment? Creating an excuse is easy; the work is the hard part. Keep reminding *yourself* that you're doing this for *you*.

> Picture this: Kelly Clarkson inspires me. Her love for singing started at an early age. Overcoming personal struggles, she won the first season of *American Idol*. Not resting on her laurels, she followed up with many chart-topping hits. Open to opportunities, her resilience is evident in her roles as a coach on *The Voice*, a national talk show host, and a spokesperson. Enduring tough times and maintaining motivation help contribute to individual success.

It's not where a person starts—it's where they end up. Put in energy, be self-honest, gain mastery, and escape your harness.

Time needs to be managed. Nothing happens by standing still. Gathering all the ingredients, mixing them together, and serving the final *pièce de résistance* takes daily effort.

Defending the statement that *I'm too busy* is another way of interrupting momentum. Admit it—as harsh as it may sound—did you make time for things that didn't advance your personal vision? I did! On the hot seat myself, I asked: Could that time have been swapped for life-enhancing projects?

Start Now: **FLIP THE SCRIPT!**

Lay out the roadmap for your specific goals. Define, refine, and set deadlines. Follow that route diligently, with flexibility. At each checkpoint, note how far you've come. Facing a detour? Recommit: Get back on course.

Be accountable: Transform what you crave into reality. Today can be the turning point. Like a train, stay on the tracks and complete your adventure. Motivation is often enhanced when paired with a sense of purpose. Devotion and stamina are the fuel.

Onward: As a barometer, when slacking off, answer these frank questions: 1. Is it worth the time? 2. Does the aim still align with my passion? If not, pivot. If it's yes, ask: Why rob myself of an exciting challenge? Confronting a problem helps ignite action.

Agree to complete your goals day by day and make it a focus.

Ready this mantra and say it with pride: *I am capable and committed to my dreams.* Don't limit the prospect of scoring a win. The decision to make it to the finish line is a choice.

In a Nutshell

* Restrain the urge—resist the next excuse; keep moving.

* Create the plan: Rally stamina and faith; live motivated.

* Step forward: Be authentic; keep mixing the ingredients.

Make Each Day Count

Someday is today; life is now, be present.

_____

The Commitment

Pay attention to the way you spend each day. Our time is finite, so why not live with intention? Vie for your heart's desire instead of just talking or thinking about it. Visualize a positive outcome, then work toward that aim. Say this out loud: Action brings it closer to reality.

_____

Do you find solace in lounging around on weekends, or after a day's work? Downtime to recharge is healthy and necessary. However, time management is key—take advantage of those extra hours, put them to good use, and work toward goals.

A personal test confirmed that lying around listlessly contributes to feeling more tired. Consider how you react and behave when you're fearful, bored, or anxiety-ridden. These emotions can act as parasites that drain creativity, resulting in exhaustion.

1. Take charge and let your destination be the inspiration. Create reminders of how good it feels to achieve your objectives. For example, post a note on the fridge.

2. Exercise releases endorphins and leaves us invigorated. The same can be said for engaging in activities that inspire us.

3. Accomplishment energizes the soul and instills pride. A mantra to spark activity: *I will do it in the present, right now. Someday is today.* Then, without hesitation, start.

Bookmark that motivated feeling; let it become the catalyst that moves you in an upward direction each day. Picture that sense of fulfillment. Begin today and shape your path.

 *Start Now*: **TAKE THE LEAP!**

Skip the calendar and jump into motion. Act with intention. Physically close all your devices and make an appearance in your life.

Even if they appear hidden and tucked away, threatening not to see daylight, what about those wishes waiting to be granted? We're the only ones who can ensure they do. Shine your light brilliantly, and release those inner desires.

Calling myself out: I control my actions. Letting go of anything non-productive makes way for what's worthwhile.

Here's a lesson in patience. As we navigate the journey of life, meaningful results often take effort and diligence to achieve. Ask yourself: What are you waiting for? Once you get started, you may find that progress happens and solutions emerge. However long it takes, invest time in your passions.

Voice in my head: Take responsibility. Now is the moment to move beyond thinking and stay the course. By combining a little planning each day with purposeful implementation, you'll be well on your way by the year's end.

In a Nutshell

* Remain accountable to yourself and practice patience.

* Each day counts. Get into motion—someday is today.

* Action! Persevere, resist non-productive distractions.

Believe You're A Gift

Action is a pathway between you and your goal.

———————————

The Commitment

Think twice about the why behind a person's motives when hurtful words become their natural response. Are they making themselves feel better by putting others down? Instead of accepting unjust remarks at face value, recognize your worth, acknowledge your talents, and be resourceful. Believe in yourself!

———————————

Maximize your superpowers—the ability is within. Live every day to the fullest. There's no one right way to secure the best life. Nobody else can do *you,* quite like *you* can.

My goals are to explore ways to fill my life with purpose and joy, to seize opportunities, give back, and nourish my soul. What dreams do you hold on to? Please, let me know.

Here's a mantra I use in pursuit of changing unhealthy habits: *You're a gift, worthy of a spectacular life.* It's important to train your mind to believe you are deserving.

> Picture this: Well before his hair and beard turned white, Colonel Harland Sanders, creator of *Kentucky Fried Chicken,* was fired from a variety of jobs. Around forty, he began cooking chicken in his roadside service station. It took years to perfect his tasty "finger lickin' good" secret recipe. He overcame many rejections before franchising, signing the first in his sixties. Trust yourself!

Often, it's clearer to see the steps necessary for improvement when looking at someone else. While viewing our own actions, proximity versus perspective may limit candid judgment, and excuses can cloud the way.

My pep talk: Uncover the truth—lasting happiness comes from within. Relying on the accolades of others to feel content and fulfilled is a self-defeating mirage. Shine an internal mirror reflecting the unique person you are.

 *Start Now*: **DITCH THE HABIT!**

Feeling insignificant? Start counting. Measure everything that brought you to this moment—the heartbeats, breaths, and processes that keep you alive. Count the teachers, friends, and investments made in you. They came together in concert. Trust in the power of you.

Hard knocks teach lessons: Learn to treat yourself with kindness—make it a priority. It shouldn't matter whether one is young or old, green behind the ears, or seasoned. Let nothing stop self-respect—not circumstances, age, or outside influences.

Here's to showing up proudly with value to offer. Allow the details to reveal *your* true intentions. Let *your* actions speak for themselves.

In a Nutshell

* Take steps to build self-trust; make feeling good a habit.

* Unwrap the gifts within—your personal superpowers.

* Maximize this one life; share all your unique qualities.

Find Your Happy Place And Live There

Embrace happiness; remain confident in who you are. Shower yourself with self-love and acceptance.

———————————

The Commitment

Adjust your approach: Identify what brings you joy, nurture it into a habit, and create a happier life.

———————————

Have you noticed that putting yourself in an uplifted state of mind can help alter the day for the better? Take into account that your viewpoint often shapes how the hours unfold.

Note: It feels so much better when we encourage positivity by owning and affirming our emotions. Cultivating self-care can help us navigate challenges and strengthen resilience.

You've probably heard the phrase *go to your happy place*. The question is: How can you get there when you're feeling down? These solutions are from personal practice.

The first technique to find a happy place was discussed in a previous step: *Walk away from negativity*. Anything negative takes up wasted, harmful room in your thoughts. Walking away creates a vacuum. Live empowered!

Here's the chance to manage your *negativity bias* and fight *self-bullying*. Allow joy to flow into all those new spaces.

The second technique is to withdraw a memory from your happiness bank. Recall an uplifting experience and make time to reflect on it. Remember the laughter, acknowledge your past wins, unlock self-pride, and welcome in upbeat thoughts.

This brings us to the third technique—get busy and stay engaged. This healthy strategy halts lingering in old harmful territory and keeps trouble at bay. Choose activities that build up confidence and stimulate future flashbacks to be proud of.

 *Start Now*: **CHANGE THINGS UP!**

> ***Design the set:* Take your time to envision the environment that will surround you in your happy zone. Why not create a joy-filled gratitude collage, schedule new happy memory makers on your calendar, or set a screensaver with cheerful images?**

Think about this: Counter negative thoughts by reframing situations to see benefits—retrieve, replay, and hug jubilant memories. Train your mind to look on the bright side; invite inner peace. The choice, followed by action, rests with us.

Research suggests that mood boosters include: 1. Happy, bright colors (yellow, orange, pink, and red) and calming, soothing colors (blue, green, and violet). 2. Humor and laughter. 3. Uplifting words and images. Energize your body and mind. A simple mantra to focus on is: *Joy, happiness, and fulfillment.*

In a Nutshell

* Add self-love. Difficult times are part of life—persevere!

* Alter your approach: Fit in happiness; include laughter.

* Infuse joyful images, happy colors, and upbeat words.

Take Breaks To Process

Now and then it's good to hit the brakes
and take time to reflect.

———————————

The Commitment

Expressing what's in your heart isn't possible without carving out time to do it. Push the pause button and then figure out the best way to proceed. Not satisfied? Why accept your life as it is? Instead, create it. The clock goes in circles; you don't have to.

———————————

Do you run and run and think you're not getting anywhere? Feeling stuck? You're not the only one. A valuable lesson: What separates the doers from time wasters is intentional action.

Have an idea? It's up to you to make it happen. Many times, a break provides answers to what's next. Control what you can.

Whether you're working to pay bills, studying to get to the next level, or doing things for family and friends, agree to dump the non-essential. Why neglect your goals?

If you're like I was, you forget to care for *yourself* and ignore *your* own desires. When you are consumed with busywork that detracts from balance, there's little time to recharge.

Up the ante: Integrate these into your to-do list. 1. Secure productivity by scratching off what's unnecessary. 2. Nourish your soul. 3. Live with passion and fulfill your dreams.

Cravings are not satiated without exiting the treadmill now and again. Take a retreat, reflect, prepare, and then get to work. Establish a schedule to best achieve your next goal. Invest time and effort!

 *Start Now:* **TAKE THE LEAP!**

Take a one-hour recess to process. Allow nothing to override this freedom. Keep in mind how good a break feels—open your calendar and build three more into the next few weeks.

My solution: Taking a breather offers time to focus on what to save or discard from the agenda. It presents the space to untangle, get inspired, and start on those next action steps.

> Picture this: While Marc Benioff worked at *Oracle*, burnout set in. He took a six-month sabbatical and used the pause to travel and reflect on opportunities in the tech world. During this hiatus, the idea for *Salesforce*, a cloud technology business to help companies better connect with their customers, was born. Create more *you-time*, and dare to dream.

Life shouldn't be torture—it should be enjoyable. Don't get bogged down. Clear out the cobwebs and embrace new beginnings. Identify and resolve what's lacking. Doing this helps me plan and take action, allowing me to leave the familiar. A mantra to inspire: *Relax, think, ignite.*

In a Nutshell

* Recharge: Get off the treadmill; create time to process.

* Satiate your cravings—don't bury them or run in circles.

* Enjoy today rather than being busy for no real gain.

Peer Through The Lens Of Optimism

Make optimism a habit—it will strengthen with use.

_____

The Commitment

Is the glass half full, or half empty? Maybe the choice is to be thankful to have a glass. Invite optimistic people into your world. They will be less likely to discourage you from making decisions that lead to a promising and purposeful life. Pour more cheer into your day.

_____

We can shape our thoughts and actions. Why not try different approaches, and evaluate the results? Stand up for your right to succeed—turn away the cynics and defeatists.

The light is trying to get in. Open the window and absorb it. How much sense does it make to set a goal, and then hold yourself back with a pessimistic view?

I'm not suggesting that everything is always possible, but if we don't seek out and explore different scenarios, the outcome will remain unknown. How can you gain a better advantage for success? Cultivate optimism, engage with it, and protect it.

Picture this: Sir Winston Churchill, known for his leadership during World War II, had many setbacks. Despite struggling in school and facing electoral defeats, his resilience ultimately led to his appointment as the United Kingdom's Prime Minister when he was in his sixties. Through it all, he proclaimed himself an optimist and never surrendered to challenges. Hold on to faith.

Optimism multiplies once you're open to it. Think about a time when you bought a new product or put it on your wish list. Then, all of a sudden, you'd see that same product everywhere. This phenomenon happens when your lens is focused tightly on a particular thought or thing.

Here's the truth—that product wasn't in the world any more or less than before. This is the power of perspective. Imagine if it could be turned on or off, fostering a fruitful life. My proof is that with the right mindset, it's possible—it's called optimism.

 *Start Now*: **FLIP THE SCRIPT!**

Are you in a pessimistic funk? Take out a photo of your younger self and write a journal entry addressed to that child in the picture. Reframe the story in a way that leaves a sense of hope. Remember to encourage yourself to feel proud!

Make today the day you expand your mind. Let your victories contribute to your rise to a bigger stage.

Nurture encouraging thoughts—it's then possibilities broaden. A pessimistic outlook can shortchange your future. Channel Churchill! Say this mantra: *I am an optimist*. Seize that spirit!

Attention: Stay on the lookout and navigate the obstacles. Why be deterred and travel under a dark cloud? Shine a light.

In a Nutshell

* Select optimism over pessimism—focus on positivity.

* Caution: Be choosy about who you spend time with.

* Break free: Leave darkness behind and seek light.

Stay Centered And Bloom

Flourish where kindness grows.
Happiness blossoms from within.

———————————

The Commitment

Focus and center—ensure goals take shape. Awaken potential. Demands on our time are many; accentuate what's essential. To achieve better results, end unproductive relationships and let go of anything that stifles growth. Don't suppress your desires!

———————————

Why not start the day on your own side? Greet the world with an upbeat disposition. Strive not to let others or their discouraging words disrupt your path. Include this mantra: *I will trust myself and appreciate the moments.*

Reading stories about people who bring their intentions to reality inspires me to be productive. Self-promise: I'll resist making endless excuses, and instead, visualize a positive outcome, get psyched up, and be proactive.

Why not be the protagonist in your life's journey? Take center stage; walk a path that exceeds even your own expectations.

Picture this: Michael Jordan, one of the greatest basketball players of all time, worked for his success. In sophomore year of high school, Jordan, not considered tall enough, didn't make the varsity team. He would tire at practice, yet push through, imagining his name missing from the list of players on the locker room wall. He centered, worked at his craft, and earned his place.

Note: If something causes misery, then it's not the right fit for you. Opt for work and activities that are enjoyable. It's absolutely worth figuring out what that is. Use a measured, well thought out approach, and align goals with talents. Keep in mind what makes you happy and bloom from the inside out.

 *Start Now*: **CHANGE THINGS UP!**

Create three columns. Title Column One: Skills. Title Column Two: What Inspires Joy? Title Column Three: Sources of Anguish. Complete each column, then circle your favorite items in Columns One and Two. In Column Three, cross off at least one issue to release.

Aha: Keep in mind what it is you want to achieve. Write it down, and keep it alive by reviewing and adjusting. If something isn't working, be flexible enough to pivot. Quench your desire's thirst—don't water it down. An old saying goes: "Opinions are like noses—everybody has one." Love yours!

Today's visual thought: You're a capable horticulturist. Plant the seeds to cultivate a fulfilling life. The bloomfest can thrive only if nurtured. Commit to tending to it and enjoy the fruits of your labor.

All the components must pull together into a lovely collage. The glue is your emotions; the more positive the better. Once it all meshes, the more likely it is to cement in place.

In a Nutshell

* Align goals with strengths—enjoyment is the objective.

* Center, bloom, and glue in place; create a beautiful life.

* Adhere to the plan; be the protagonist in your journey.

Stop Wasting Your Time

Allow yourself to soar; let go of
the things that hold you back.

———————

The Commitment

Treat each day thoughtfully and respectfully. Much of life's success can be influenced by our thoughts and actions. The choice to do something is as important as the decision not to.

———————

Are you guilty of wasting precious time? Is it limiting your future plans? If so, sincere request: Why not be honest and self-aware, exit the loop, and turn onto a better path?

My inspirational mantra: *I will make a decision to live with intent, passion, and self-respect.*

Do you often feel like you're flitting around without order? If so, think about spending time on what's important.

Truthful evaluation: Ever wonder how your habits got started in the first place? Look at your activity, reexamine your thoughts, and assess with candor. Adjust and improve by addressing what's in the way. Structure a productive routine.

When unforeseen events occur or situations don't pan out as planned, instead of fretting and being self-critical, I accept that I did my best. The energy I save by not worrying frees me to try again with a different method.

Picture this: I applaud Julie Powell's story, made famous in *Julie & Julia*. Her mother reminds her that *she doesn't finish projects*. Powell overcame her mom's concern by cooking a Julia Child recipe almost every day and blogging about each adventure. The blog became very successful, earning Julie a book and movie deal—a testament to her hard work. She empowered herself by following a plan and showing her mother a different outcome.

Think about this: Why give up, or head in a direction that doesn't resonate with your heart and gut? Action item: Don't block out the potential to make a positive difference.

 *Start Now*: **DITCH THE HABIT!**

Stand in front of a mirror and ask yourself: 1. Am I wasting my time on meaningless activities? 2. Are they detracting from my goals? If so, respond out loud with one way to correct the issue and agree to the change. Visit the mirror and use this exercise whenever procrastination arises.

Destination upward: Life's a journey; live and enjoy. It's a creation in progress to be embraced. Time isn't an unlimited resource—use with care. Make a promise to go the extra mile.

Quit now: Are you crowding the day with tasks that rob your time? Not all busy is equal. It's Pareto's Principle: "For many outcomes, roughly 80% of consequences come from 20% of causes."

In a Nutshell

* Be hyper-aware of how you spend time—don't waste it.

* Make it a habit: Own productivity; release distractions.

* Assess and adjust your routine—rid the busywork.

Things To Remember:

Take action! Motivate yourself—make each day meaningful. Toast your life. Believe in the power of you and spread your gifts outward. Make it a habit to retrieve, replay, and savor joyful memories as a counter to negativity. Create time to take breaks and reflect. Uncover your happy place and live at that address. Exercise optimism! Center and bloom; have faith the best is yet to come. Carefully choose where you focus your attention. Ditch busy work, prioritize tasks, and use time wisely—don't waste it. Now, give yourself some love.

* Call to action: Motivation isn't as hard as you may fear.

* Set an alarm as your reminder to make every day count.

* Appreciate yourself—you're unique. Share all your gifts.

* Uplift your mood and discover a happy, calm place.

* When you're stuck, hit pause, and figure out next steps.

* Reflect: Take breaks to process—stay flexible and enjoy.

* Support this habit: Live life through an optimistic lens.

* Take center stage; become the protagonist in your life.

* Align your goals with your strengths—savor the choices.

* Manage time: 20% of most efforts yield 80% of results.

Thoughts:

_____

_____

_____

_____

_____

_____

_____

_____

_____

_____

_____

_____

_____

_____

_____

_____

_____

_____

_____

_____

_____

Motivational Checklist: Visit thedailydecisions.com/inspire

Live life your way! Don't just blend in, stand out. Create the life you envision.

Anecdote:

Leaving design behind and landing a job as a sales rep, I began a new chapter. I was told it takes years to become a top salesperson, but I was able to achieve success within a year by aligning my attitude with my intentions.

My delight in being helpful, combined with a positive outlook and dedication to building customer trust, established me as a top performer despite any obstacles.

I learned many lessons. Here are some: People have their agendas, don't take things personally, maintain self-belief, remain in control, stay away from gossip, and persevere.

Step 5: The Attitude

Think about this: Responses, aligned with attitude, shape the outcome of a situation. Things may not happen as expected or work to plan—how they're handled makes the end result better or worse.

Remaining confident and open to options, managing feelings of defeat, and not giving in to uncomplimentary chatter are better choices for overall well-being.

Key Takeaway:

Successful people have faith in their abilities—this belief often leads to better outcomes. Conversely, those who are easily discouraged may find it harder to persist.

Self-assurance, tenacity, fortitude, and confidence are helpful assets when dealing with challenges, disappointments, and setbacks.

Positivity can open doors, while negativity might close them. The choice is yours to make. Look inward and be truthful. Do you want something? Coordinate your goals with a can-do attitude and work for the results.

It's About The Attitude

Give yourself an attitude upgrade
and turn negatives into positives.

_____

The Commitment

Instead of underestimating the power of your outlook, remember that self-belief can help boost the chances of success. A positive, confident attitude can elevate results, and regular reality checks help clear the way for true potential. Make the choice.

_____

Are your disruptive thoughts the culprit? Do they interrupt, compromise, and steal what could have been a pleasant day?

Self-correct: Manage negative thoughts before they begin to stir up feelings of insecurity. Counter that thinking and replace it with a productive approach.

Note: Over time, I've found that unproven, poisonous beliefs rile up emotions, undermine progress, and lessen the chances for positive endings. So, why do that to yourself?

> Picture this: Creating a path and walking it with determination reminds me of how the company, *Baked by Melissa*, got its start. Losing a job led to opportunity.

> After being fired from a New York City advertising agency, Melissa Ben-Ishay turned her love of baking into a business with the support of those around her. Her signature mini cupcakes bring smiles to everyone who sees, buys, and enjoys them.

Anger, stress, negativity, or fear—whichever it is that ruins the moment—if allowed to fester, can strangle better results.

The aftermath of toxic emotions is harmful, unfavorably impacting all involved. My truce: Rather than apologizing later, I manage the reaction before it escalates.

It gets easier with practice. Speaking from experience, no matter how difficult it may be to squelch bad behavior and prevent heat from rising, it helps melt away the destructive habits that hold back creativity and successful results.

 *Start Now*: **CHANGE THINGS UP!**

> **Each day, do a morning mood check and modify as needed. Test out these suggestions to keep anger in check: 1. Breathe. 2. Count to ten. 3. Anticipate the chain reaction and intervene before it starts. 4. Set an intended objective weekly.**

A mantra to inspire confidence: *I've got this!* The secret is to act on those words.

A positive attitude is a helpful part of living an intentional life. It can change any day for the better—every moment, month, year, and relationship. Check in, live connected, walk your path with an open mind, and make every day the best it can be. Greet a life you love!

In a Nutshell

* Manage your attitude; prevent more downward spirals.

* Become known for your self-confidence and positivity.

* Shut out the poisons—reach for hidden possibilities.

Live With Gratitude And Grace

Open your heart!
Extend a hand and inspire compassion.

———————

The Commitment

Adopt this as a mantra: Be kind to others. Before speaking your mind, remember people need and respond to kindness. Everyone wants to be heard and respected. Treat each person the way you wish to be treated. Lead with appreciation.

———————

Why not be a positive force? Don't good vibes feel better? Helping others can be the best medicine when feeling down. Many times, simple things have the most enriching impact.

Notice how the energy rebounds and your mood shifts for the better when helping someone else. Science suggests that a genuinely selfless act can stimulate the brain's reward center.

Paying it forward doesn't have to cost anything. I've witnessed that simply walking someone across the street and receiving a smile of gratitude can flip around a less-than-optimal day.

When you do something kind, it often boomerangs back when least expected. What you put out reflects back like a mirror.

A humble, appreciative attitude can effectively help us let go of negative thoughts, spark positive ones, cultivate good karma, and foster a pulse-pumping sense of pride.

Did you know? Anger can cause chest tightening, shortness of breath, and loss of control. Gratitude is the reverse, triggering lovely warmth and a grounded, happy, content feeling.

 *Start Now*: **FLIP THE SCRIPT!**

Stay in touch with your appreciation and gratitude, and think about doing an unplanned spur-of-the-moment act of kindness. Give time or food, and share your kind words and laughter.

A good deed from the heart can help release toxic emotions and make way for joy to enter. Make it social—invite others to join. Choose safely and resist adding extra pressure.

Add your special touch. Here's some inspiration: Jean Paul Laurent founded *Unspoken Smiles*, a nonprofit dedicated to promoting better oral health for at-risk children worldwide.

Studies indicate that smiling makes us more attractive and likable. Although it may seem counterintuitive, practicing altruism during challenging times—not just when life is going your way—can bring self-satisfaction and yield meaningful rewards.

Practice kindness toward yourself, help others, and spread goodness. Leave a lasting mark—share your heart. Exchanging compassion can be uplifting and fulfilling.

In a Nutshell

* Live with gratitude and grace, topped with goodwill.

* The simplest kind acts offer rich, feel-good rewards.

* Show respect: Be nice to yourself and to others.

Be Present – Open To Possibilities

When you leave what feels safe
and try something new, you discover
what you're capable of achieving.

The Commitment

Stay flexible and engaged. Live in the moment. Listen for clues. Always remain receptive to promising possibilities that may arise. Redirect as necessary to prevent anything from blocking your way.

Now, not whenever! Are you just existing? Why not live the life you imagine? Shine brightly—don't sit on the sidelines.

Have you ever been in a situation where you wanted to achieve one thing, but it just wasn't happening? Welcome a new vision, bravely pivot, and embrace the learning curve.

Remember: Why be shortchanged? Capture opportunities. How? Choose an open mind instead of pre-judging whether someone or something will or won't enhance your life.

Helping hand: Someone's good intentions might arrive at the right time and become your blessing. Listen to supportive advice with clarity and without judgment. Trust your instincts. Trial and error can lead to effective results.

Live in the present moment—be open to possibilities. Confront your fears and persist in the face of adversity. Why live in a bubble? Ask for help and accept only what feels right.

Picture this: Rachael Ray charms us with a bubbly personality. Growing up around restaurants, food became a calling. She did cooking demonstrations on local TV and published a cookbook before her life-changing break came, when *The Today Show* called. Arriving during a snowstorm and acing the segment, *Food Network* and talk show executives took notice. Shape a life you love.

Shift: Look for the silver lining, even on a difficult day. Find joy in stressful moments; be positive and self-kind, even when doubtful. Attitude choice makes a problem better or worse.

Turn obstacles into opportunities: Upon reflection, I've found that when facing a challenging situation, jumping into the driver's seat and being flexible makes it easier to bypass barriers. Leave your comfort zone and pave a new way.

 *Start Now*: **TAKE THE LEAP!**

> **Set your intent: Determine a specific goal and write it down on multiple small slips of paper. Place one on your nightstand, carry another one with you, and post it where it can be seen. Focus on your goal and put in effort. Keep an open mind—let your vision unfold.**

Self-reminder: A receptive attitude can help to level up any day. Incorporate an abundance mentality! Trust that there are plenty of opportunities for everyone. Endorse this mantra: *I have what it takes—affirmed.* Open your arms and accept challenges.

In a Nutshell

* Be present and ready to welcome in life's possibilities.

* Seek out and uncover the silver lining on a tough day.

* Star in your own life—don't hide in the background.

Don't Take The Bait

The path to success is shaped by our choices and how we respond to obstacles.

_____

The Commitment

Don't let anyone egg you on. Refuse to get whipped into a froth. No drama or annoying nonsense allowed! Maintain your composure, no matter what's said. You are in control of your reactions.

_____

Why do people like to push our buttons? Is it a game to gain a personal edge? Does it make them feel better or superior? Whatever the reason, instead of trying to figure it out, ignore it and go about your day without constant worry or engaging in nonsense. Use this mantra: *I will protect my dignity.*

The minute I stopped overthinking, anticipating what others would do, or projecting what might happen, my output was no longer crippled. My firm decision not to let internal criticism interfere with my goals quieted negative inner chit-chat.

My solution: Resist succumbing to those petty things people say. Clue: Is what they're saying truthful? If it is, take in those helpful suggestions and use them to grow stronger. If not, move on, block it out, and shake off the sting. Develop a thick skin.

Remain mindful of the difference between what is said by one person and what is really believed by others. Let your own good attitude set the tone and represent you.

Picture this: *Charlie Brown* and *Peanuts* creator Charles Schulz had his share of challenges. He failed eighth grade and didn't excel at sports. To top it off, Schulz's drawings were rejected by the high school yearbook staff. Even as a young adult, his cartoon submissions were turned down by *Disney*. Overcoming the hurt and sharing the human angst that we feel in his characters led to success. Stand firm and follow your path. Celebrate your own gifts.

I can attest that nothing positive results from becoming inflamed due to a bruised ego. It's counterproductive and drains energy. The prospect of losing a friendship was my wake-up call to think before reacting. I chose not to get worked up, take a step back, and control my reaction.

 *Start Now*: **DITCH THE HABIT!**

Bait the hook of your dreams. Carry a photo (in your phone or wallet) that reflects the ideal you. If someone is trying your patience, quickly use that photo as a *best-you* boost, and a mindful pause.

My secret: A hidden smile as I exit, without having taken the bait. Rather than opening the floor and giving away the upper hand, turn the corner, create a graceful bow-out, and clear the air. It becomes easier each time you change the mood.

Fresh start: Assess before reacting and conserve your energy. Make the decision not to turn over your power.

In a Nutshell

* Safeguard your integrity; no drama allowed—resist it.

* Develop a thick skin; refuse to get worked up. Smile!

* Avoid letting anyone push your buttons—own it.

Positivity – Positivity – Positivity

A positive attitude is infectious;
be the source. Spread it around freely.

The Commitment

Red light to anyone who tries to spoil even a moment of your day. Give a green light to a positive outlook and lifestyle. Focus on being confident, gentle, and thoughtful when representing yourself. Keep courage in motion and spirits elevated.

Has bitterness spread its noxious fumes, robbed glee, and killed aspirations? Why not agree to release anything that gets in the way of your passion? A mantra to cultivate the desired attitude: *Resist negativity and embrace positivity.*

Self-care message: Take measures to sustain a healthy point of view. Allow your internal light to radiate outward. Attitude choice rests within.

In the past, one thing could throw me off balance, put me in a bad mood, or disrupt my focus. I learned to distract myself and halt those unsettling thoughts. Why let emotions ruin the day and upset your peace? Own it and guide your direction.

It's a disservice to yourself to suffer. So, why get wrapped up in the nasty comments of others, accept what the imagination suggests, or allow unpleasant thoughts to become all-consuming? Answer is: It's a mind shift!

The ability to offset letdowns with pick-me-ups helps keep emotions in check, even in difficult situations. I've experienced that nurturing an optimistic state of mind is the charm.

Goals and emotional well-being are simpler to achieve when cultivating a supportive atmosphere. Each challenge becomes easier to handle with practice. Positivity attracts positivity.

 *Start Now*: **CHANGE THINGS UP!**

Begin each day with an uplifting affirmation. Have a collection and rotate them. During the day, when you need encouragement, say one out loud. This solution can help block toxic chatter from entering your mind.

Personal discovery: Manage those pesky thoughts. By adjusting my perspective and channeling good energy, I lessen dread, so the day begins and ends in the best possible way.

Think about this: Attitude rules! While in college, Kevin Plank faced a personal need. Cotton t-shirts weren't an ideal sweat absorber under his football jersey. An urge to develop a moisture-wicking shirt—his passion project and side hustle—birthed *Under Armour*. Stop complaining. Find your solution.

A template for your attitude: You're exuding positive energy and others feel it. The universe aligns. Craft your outlook for favorable change. Contentment is a by-product.

In a Nutshell

* Synchronize your attitude to nurture success—practice.

* Positivity boosts results; the energy radiates outward.

* Enhance your story; thoughts shape the narrative.

What You Think Matters

Believe in the power of your thoughts;
they contribute to the end result.

———————————

The Commitment

Pause before buying into and accepting criticism that negates your opinion. It's not okay! Gather self-conviction and take a stand. What you think matters. Rally inner power and don't be defined. Distance yourself from anyone who disrupts your confidence.

———————————

Make a choice: Be front and center in your life. Why remain convinced that an idea won't work before giving it a try? Where's the cold, hard evidence? Uh-huh—time to take the leap.

Staying true to yourself can help weather challenges more effectively. Why let others' negativity hold you back from achieving your goals? Instead, choose to keep moving ahead.

Keep this in mind: Once I committed body and soul to the worthiness of my views, it became easier to push past the noise, and see projects through to completion.

Empowerment note: 1. I'll strive to be open-minded, observe, and listen for suggestions that may offer solutions. 2. I won't echo a voice that doesn't feel right or abandon my heartfelt pursuits. 3. I'll speak my truth.

Accomplishments provide strength to speak up again and again.

Dr. Seuss was turned down over twenty times before he got a deal. Actor Harrison Ford was told he wouldn't succeed. *Star Wars* and *Indiana Jones* fans would disagree. And, Jay-Z? No label would sign him, prompting him to start his own.

My antidote: A sincere pep talk. Everyone faces rejection. Words to encourage: *I will tap into inner belief and manage fear.*

 *Start Now*: **FLIP THE SCRIPT!**

> **Remind yourself of a time you voiced an idea or opinion in a group, and people sat up, listened, and found value in your message. Write a quote that corresponds with that experience and use it as a morale booster when you feel uncertain.**

Unite with determination and bravery. Take them along everywhere. Keep them close; fight the impulse to let nerves rattle the bond. Live courageously and become unstoppable.

Fear of failure is a reason we may give up. Why be another casualty? Stand up for yourself, your ideas, and values. Share this mantra: *My talents are needed.* Believe it!

Despite being told something wasn't possible, I find that simply trying can invite helpful results. My agreement: Buckle down, confront doubt, and follow through on what's important to you. Confidence and courage go hand in hand.

In a Nutshell

* Embrace rejection: Learn from it! Improve—keep going.

* Rise: Be your own champion—push through the noise.

* Incorporate this: Trust that what you think matters.

Give Yourself Your Stamp Of Approval

Make life simpler; stop complicating it.
Adjust your attitude and reach your destination.

––––––––––

The Commitment

Let your true worth and know-how shine. Believe that what you have to share is worthy of consideration. Ignite it with conviction and pride. Start the day with a personal stamp of approval.

––––––––––

Why not pat yourself on the back for past, present, and future jobs well done? Display backbone and grit. Trust that what you serve up deserves to be heard and has value.

My decision: Learn from mistakes, setbacks, and successes—both mine and others. Picture life as a triathlon. Never stop stretching. Self-belief extends outward. I repeat, my choice is to rename the word failure, and call it education.

The ability to zig and zag—being adaptable—is helpful. If you're truly convinced you're on the right track, why give up? Keep training, listen, evaluate, and adjust what needs improvement.

Keep the feeling of past wins at the forefront of your mind. When challenged, fire up the memory, and trust yourself.

My mantra to keep the faith: *I'm validated—stamp approved.* Dare to bring your vision to life; combine devotion and effort.

Picture this: *Starbucks'* founder Howard Schultz was turned down by investors over two hundred times, but never lost hope.

Vital message: The moment is now! Carve out time—don't waste it. Work, achieve, and be productive. Live your life's vision.

Self-acceptance is the hurdle. Trust that your strength lies within, and develop resilience. Attitude can be an important factor that influences our path toward personal success—or limits it.

A setback doesn't mean give up; it means get up, brush yourself off, and move forward. Proudly pursue the life you desire with the confidence that you can shape its direction.

 *Start Now*: **TAKE THE LEAP!**

Imagine a sheet of stickers—the ones that say: Amazing! Congratulations! Way to go! Visualize sticking one on to bump up your self-esteem. Celebrate each step forward—remember you are enough.

Whenever you feel there's more to achieve, or doing better is possible, think of life as a series of games—some are won, others lost. Unlock those valuable lessons and keep learning.

Use my approach: Simply do your best and step into a bigger version of yourself.

In a Nutshell

* Appear at your finest—no apologies for a job well done.

* Own the power: Stand proud; pat yourself on the back.

* Stamp approved—don't let anyone steal your thunder.

Satisfaction Comes From Within

When everything feels like an uphill climb,
envision the view from the peak.

————————

The Commitment

Adopting a resilient attitude can often be a more effective approach when facing misfortune and distress. Include it when working to prevail over hardships. Shape a positive future and a fulfilled life.

————————

Has it been difficult to believe in yourself? Do you give up when the going gets tough? Take a moment to reflect when facing adversity. Advocate for yourself with care and understanding.

You're the master craftsman of your life; treat and regard it as your most cherished project.

Keep in mind the thousands of hours needed to achieve mastery and don't be discouraged when mistakes happen on the way to refining your dream life. Welcome in new knowledge.

My strategy: Developing the habit of blocking out venomous thoughts was my ticket to freedom. By facing the destructive voices, forbidding them to sneak in and linger, and declaring a zero tolerance policy, I found the courage to take action.

If reading this on an off day, you might say: Rubbish—that's not possible! Challenge that instinct before discrediting the strategy. Test it out and see what you can achieve.

Reminder: Attitude and actions play a part in the outcome. Rustle up a smile on your face and fire in that belly—everything is easier when you decide to be on your own side.

Satisfaction comes from within. It's self-defeating to compare your beginning to someone else's finale. Compliment both big and small triumphs. Go ahead: Clap for yourself.

How about this? The mantra starts with the sound of clapping, followed by the words: *I'm proud of myself.* Now, take a bow.

 *Start Now*: **DITCH THE HABIT!**

Instead of harsh criticism, honor and commend yourself. Plan a party just for you. Make a celebratory meal. Bake a cake and feel special. Embrace your worth!

Here's a solution: 1. Express gratitude for the simple things, such as a sunrise. 2. Welcome success without guilt and believe you deserve it. 3. Focus on the positive and self-praise to encourage and inspire confidence. You'll be leagues ahead.

Simply start: 1. Recognize your abilities. 2. Don't compare. 3. Own all achievements. 4. Reevaluate relationships and set boundaries. 5. Explore drawing contentment from within.

Practice: 1. Self-trust. 2. Step boldly out of the comfort zone. 3. Follow your ambitions. 4. Bravely, think big.

In a Nutshell

* Push through challenges and confidently lead your day.

* Nourish peace of mind; cultivate a sense of tranquility.

* Calm disruptive thoughts; unite your life with courage.

Things To Remember:

It's about the attitude! Positivity is a helpful friend. Be kind, compassionate, and patient with yourself. Live with gratitude and grace—open to life's possibilities. Reflect before giving in to fear or allowing disruptive, negative words to rob your future. Exit your comfort zone with confidence and optimism. What you think matters. Stamp approved! Work toward those dreams. Set boundaries, stop comparing, and reevaluate relationships. Safeguard your integrity; no drama allowed—block it out. Onward and upward. Satisfaction is the ticket.

* Attitude check: Trade a negative thought for a positive.

* Commit to gratitude and appreciation; live with grace.

* Be kind: Treat others the way you'd like to be treated.

* Remain open to possibilities; reach your full potential.

* Star in your life! Don't take the bait or shush your voice.

* Enhance your story; thoughts shape the narrative.

* Reflect positively: Why put yourself down? You matter.

* Develop a thick skin; nurture and craft a fulfilling life.

* Self-advocate: Courageously give yourself a green light.

* Contentment comes from within; hug your inner gifts.

Thoughts:

_____

_____

_____

_____

_____

_____

_____

_____

_____

_____

_____

_____

_____

_____

_____

_____

_____

_____

_____

_____

_____

_____

Happiness Worksheet: Visit thedailydecisions.com/inspire

Don't let your problems be an excuse to give up on heartfelt dreams.

Anecdote:

This book has taken a long time to write. I persevered with determination, even when I faced challenging moments. The steps and lessons are straight from my personal guidebook and outline common struggles. I broke it down simply, added pep talks to overcome bad habits, and cheered for the grit needed to achieve goals.

The daily decisions we make to push through and stay engaged aren't easy, but they help foster growth.

I find that when I question myself or feel a lack of commitment, rereading the applicable parts of this book helps jump-start action. Writing notes on the lined pages at the end of each step reinforces my understanding.

Step 6: The Commitment

Word of honor: Stay focused and true to your values. Don't surrender before trying (keep going, *Dorothy*). Change is constant. Develop, advance, and flourish. Building self-trust helps to encourage positive momentum. Never let others break your will; you're deserving (take that, *Wicked Witch*).

Make time for that special something in your heart (shout-out to you, *Tin Man*). Commit to a confident outlook, believe in yourself, and, with courage (yes, you, *Cowardly Lion*), persist and power through.

Key Takeaway:

Remain alert! Problems shouldn't become an excuse to abandon *your* objectives. Resist the temptation.

Why quit now and look back with regret years later?

1. Fight distractions and laziness. Manage disapproval, stay determined, and put in the effort.

2. Face fear! Give yourself some love—be your loyal fan. Steadily work toward what's important to you.

3. Allow progress to be the stimulant that keeps your juices flowing. You have the potential to reach your goals with the right focus and effort. Commit, don't concede.

Remember To Be Grateful

Satisfaction is not only about fulfilling our wants;
it's also about appreciating what we already have.

––––––––––––

The Commitment

*Stop whining! Don't complain, do the opposite: Give thanks for
what you do have, work for the rest, and be open to life's blessings.*

––––––––––––

Is there something you want—a promotion at work, a special
job, an item you can't afford, or a million and one other shiny
desires—but it's just not happening? Reset and instead, enjoy
today. Find something to be grateful for, and try, try again.

A mantra to inspire gratitude: *I will count my blessings*. Have
faith, no matter how daunting—stay committed. Look for the
silver lining; believe greener pastures lie ahead.

We all experience the good, the bad, and sometimes the horrific. On occasion, there's no avoiding it. Loved ones depend
on us—trust that you can push through.

Gratitude helps: a. Increase optimism. b. Positively impact
overall health. c. Strengthen relationships. d. Bolster self-
esteem. e. Rid bitterness. f. Cope with stress. g. Experience
joy and comfort. Unwrap your magic—blessings are all around.

1. Jealousy harms the spirit. 2. Resentment kills creativity.
3. Comparisons? Avoid. 4. Your uniqueness? Appreciate.

Self-reminder ABCs: Science suggests that when the brain's neurotransmitters (dopamine and serotonin) increase, they trigger positive feelings in proportion to our elevated degrees of: A. Gratitude. B. Happiness. C. Contentment. Greet feel-good vibes. Frequency is what creates habit.

 *Start Now*: **CHANGE THINGS UP!**

> Start a *Why I'm Grateful Jar.* Grab a piece of paper, write I am thankful for _____, and drop it in. Let the appreciation multiply as the jar fills up. In difficult situations, reach in for inspiration to boost your spirits.

Tip: Helping others can uplift both the recipient and the giver. It allows for pause, which creates a lens to notice the light. Partake in magical moments of joy. See the good as a blanket of comfort in times of angst.

> Picture this: Here's some next-level gratitude. I heard a story about a seventy-four-year-old woman who felt lucky to receive a donor kidney when family members weren't a match. Only four weeks after her mom's surgery, her daughter, so determined to show thanks, donated a kidney to a thirty-five-year-old man who had been on a waiting list for five years. Blessings circulate.

Note to self: I choose not to feel entitled or superior. I prefer to remain humble and hopeful. Rather than looking for something in return, I believe the gift is in the giving.

In a Nutshell

* Cancel out jealousy: Give of yourself instead; be a blessing.

* When times are tough, find ways to sweeten what's bitter.

* Be thankful, grateful, appreciative, not resentful, or cruel.

Never Cause Yourself Harm

What limits us is the doubt
in our own inner strength.

The Commitment

You are your most important resource. Take time to nourish body, mind, and spirit—live at your best. Never engage in self-abuse or accept mistreatment from others. Send welcoming thoughts out to the world every day. Appreciate the gifts that return.

Why wouldn't you treat yourself with the ultimate respect and care? Many people find ways to derail themselves from reaching their potential, going in the wrong direction, or following others on a slippery slope. Defend your dignity and honor your value. Choose self-compassion.

1. *Motivation boost*: Stay strong, live proud, and lead by example. Invite those who complement, not detract.

2. *Cultivate this*: Strive for harmony in all aspects of your life. Reconcile with this important puzzle piece and keep it in mind. Remember, you have helpful contributions to offer.

3. *Confidence check*: How dare you mistreat yourself or become someone else's scapegoat? Self-advocate!

4. *Balance tip*: Give and take appropriately—be careful not to deplete the energy needed to walk your road in full force.

5. *Build resilience:* Not everything will work out. Summon up a non-stick mentality and brush the hurt off.

 *Start Now:* **TAKE THE LEAP!**

> **Be your own cheerleader. List three or four things that make you wonderful. Hold them close and use them as an antidote to pessimism—yours or someone else's—whenever it emerges.**

Add a sense of humor and don't take yourself so seriously. I've found that meeting my own expectations improves when I keep that in mind.

My jump-start: Awaken the inner navigator and get off the struggle bus. A mantra for today: *Living my best life includes being kind to myself.* Make it a daily decision.

Stand strong: I will tap into my strength, as an ally, not an adversary. Consider this: At fifteen, Charlize Theron witnessed her mother shoot her alcoholic father in self-defense. Theron chose to channel energy into acting, becoming the first South African actress to win an Academy Award. Accept, heal, soar.

Think about this: Make it a rule to start each day with words of love and encouragement. Move beyond your past and shame, guilt, doubt, grudges, or negativity. Instead of self-punishing—hug yourself. Create your happily ever after.

In a Nutshell

* Get off the struggle bus; embrace balance and harmony.

* Reject harmful words or abuse—don't be a scapegoat.

* Remember, you're important; be your own kind friend.

Spin Your World Beautiful

Appreciate yesterday. Live today. Own tomorrow.

The Commitment

No matter how bad the day is, it's vital to have hope and live with faith. Instead of letting a stumbling block cloud your outlook for future potential, focus on finding solutions. Keep calm and carry on.

Life can be exhausting. Are there times when you've just had enough? Take a breath. Remember all the good experiences. It's easy to say and hard to do, but helpful to be content.

Self-discovery: We create our own happiness. When faced with painful and stressful situations, it's possible to manage negative thoughts with consistent practice and effort.

Make the choice: A better way to cope is not to wallow. Instead, alter your mindset to flip the day around; create positive vibes. Think first—I'll use self-love and care for myself.

Seize the present. Are you feeling sorry for yourself? Life should be cherished, not dreaded. When unfortunate events cause upset, look for a rainbow. Participate in your change—be receptive to opportunity. Allow the sweet to follow the bitter.

Conquer your day: As hard as it may be to work through emotions in moments of sadness, anger, or when unexpected interruptions come out of left field, looking for solutions gets us back in the game faster than living under a dark cloud.

My fix: In difficult times, it helps to maintain restraint. It's wise to stay alert, take a pause, and center before reacting.

 *Start Now*: **FLIP THE SCRIPT!**

> *Reflect on this motto credited to writer Elbert Hubbard:* **"When life gives you lemons, make lemonade!"** *Recollect those tart moments and recall how you reacted. Was there a way to switch it up by adding sugar?*

Picture this: While surfing in Kauai, thirteen-year-old Bethany Hamilton's left arm was completely bitten off by a shark. The horrific incident, followed by surgery, didn't stop Bethany from living her dream. In fact, she never allowed the terrifying event to diminish her spirit. She was back on her surfboard in a month, and about two years later, competed in the *National Scholastic Surfing Association* championships.

Self-reset: No one can do *us* like *we* can. Take ownership of the future. Simply do *your* best.

Focus on what can be accomplished; live life to the fullest. My mantra: *Today has so much to offer—I bring positive energy.*

Make it intentional: Inhale and exhale; invite passion into all that potential. Allow each breath to match the intended desire.

Make it official: Get out there! Guided by meaningful living, kindle those heartfelt aspirations. Give them wings to fly.

In a Nutshell

* Paint the world in your style; be yourself. Seize the day!

* Cherish lovely moments; don't give in to difficult times.

* Turn lemons into lemonade and create a fulfilling life.

Illuminate Your Inner Flame

One way to achieve your vision lies in
nurturing the inner fire that fuels your passions.

_____

The Commitment

Objectives may work, morph, and evolve. It's yours to construct. Take a leap of faith and embrace the unknown. Secure a healthy, happy life. Shine from the inside so that your light radiates outward.

_____

Do you find that you snuff out your inner fire before sparks erupt, smothering your chances to burn brightly? A mantra to uplift today: *I choose to seek the opportunities ahead.*

The first step: Use your personal flair and X factor to drive change. Permit your well-being to always be first choice.

The next step: Entice a bright outlook; add a healthy mind and spirit. Passion is the tinder that sparks and ignites your light.

Continue with: Take time to reset and recharge; reclaim your energy. The visual: Stoke your embers—strive for balance and be careful not to burn out.

Follow through: Put in effort—it's the gasoline on the flame that fires up your commitment. Discourage fear, distractions, stalling tactics, and criticism from becoming an interruption.

Why give up and settle? Aim to bring your best self each day.

Consider this: Nurture passion and show heart. Test out what uplifts you and blend it with your life's choices.

 *Start Now*: **CHANGE THINGS UP!**

Why complicate today? Write down three things that you did effortlessly. Appreciate your achievements. Rather than reinventing the wheel, rinse and repeat a successful method. Recreate it. Pulse vibrant energy into the next challenge, not exhaustion.

Blake Mycoskie, founder of *TOMS*, is a compassionate entrepreneur. His model was to donate a pair of shoes for each one sold. He suffered burnout, which inspired an interest in well-being and mental health. It sparked a new venture, *Madefor*, a subscription service to promote wellness. Ignite your life!

Have you encouraged family, friends, and co-workers to care for themselves? Why not add daily self-care and rejuvenate yourself? Whether the goal is to buy a home, take a trip, start a business, or volunteer—do it with your well-being in mind.

When your stamina is waning, enlist those same supporters to return the favor. An inner circle can be a bellows to keep the fire aglow. Welcome an accountability partner, reward system, or mentor to help cultivate a healthy productive life.

Believe in yourself; fuel your life's flame. Seek a path to thrive.

In a Nutshell

* Stick to your commitment—add personal flair and shine.

* Bet on yourself. Avoid burnout; instead, spark a light.

* Ignite your well-being; don't snuff out your inner fire.

Exude Sunshine - Light The Way

**A warm and genuine smile
offers a beautiful gift of kindness.**

The Commitment

Make a habit of beginning and ending the day with positivity, hope, and gratitude. Think before acting. Resist what doesn't feel right.

Do you find that a single disruptive event can throw off your balance, hinder the day's flow, and bring on a foul mood? Aha, who's running this show? Staying aware, controlling triggers, and focusing on well-being helps to enjoy life.

Add some sparkle—commit to a kind gesture. Your sense of fulfillment will far outweigh the time it takes to be nice and express empathy. The gratification returned is the reward.

Reveal the light: Stay present, engage, and practice grace and understanding toward yourself. Rather than ignoring someone else's woes, find moments to be selfless.

Live to the fullest: Surround yourself with pleasant people who bring out your best, and extend a helping hand in return.

My personal remodel: 1. Expose a sensitive side. 2. Choose to be considerate. 3. Make a meaningful difference. 4. Highlight goodwill. 5. Smile from the heart. If everyone practiced kindness, think about the impact it would have.

Honest talk: Rude and mean is hurtful and can't be retracted. After witnessing the consequences of my disruptive actions, or those of others, I've found that it never ends well. My choice: Spread compassion. Rise to the occasion; lift someone up.

Be a driving force—a voice for positive change. Help to navigate challenging situations for yourself and those in your circle.

 *Start Now*: **DITCH THE HABIT!**

Remember a rude comment that you or someone else made. Take a little time to think about the feelings it stirred. Use this memory to avoid being a part of that behavior again.

Think about this: Jacqueline Way encouraged her children's happiness through an act of giving every day. It started with her youngest donating blankets to a local animal shelter. Her *365give* became a movement. Kindness invites happiness.

Love not hate: The world sometimes feels like a cold place. A caring action coupled with a tender heart warms things up.

Take note: Manage resentment and replace it with acceptance. No matter how hard life gets, it's better to find a path to entice hope, not diminish it. A mantra to help trust in the process: *My why will guide the way.*

In a Nutshell

* Light the way: Be a shining example; spread goodwill.

* Show your empathy; add sunshine to someone's day.

* Live happier: Replace negative energy with altruism.

Acknowledge Your Accomplishments

Pause and celebrate yourself for a
job well done. Don't wait for others to do it.

_____

The Commitment

Take ownership and acknowledge your unique self. Hold firm and avoid letting anyone convince you otherwise. Select a winner mentality and stand tall. Don't forfeit that right.

_____

What's wrong with walking with a little swagger? Nothing! Why be so hard on yourself? After living up to your personal best, own your value. Self-belief, coupled with support and trust, is an effective combination.

My realization: There's a reason people spread nasty gossip. Before taking criticism to heart, ask yourself this: Was that snide remark a mechanism to bolster their self-esteem and affirm their worth?

Think of life as a series of tests. Learn, grow, and rise. Verbalizing our triumphs helps build confidence and creates self-satisfaction. Simply believe in your abilities.

Picture this: Entrepreneur Sir Richard Branson motivates me to embrace self-belief. He pushed through, dyslexia and all. Leaning on his strength and willing to think big, take risks, and weather mistakes propelled his _Virgin Group_ to the apex. Success in travel, health, space exploration, financial services, music, and other ventures is proof that nice people do finish first.

Self-acceptance will get you further than belittling yourself. When you're hesitant, remember a moment in your life when continuing on, despite your fear, was beneficial. Let that be your encouragement to keep going.

Agree to stay committed. Why bow out? When doubt lurks and your follow through is in question, ask yourself: Will I have regrets in the future?

 *Start Now:* **FLIP THE SCRIPT!**

What would you give yourself credit for? What actions shouldn't be repeated? Use the answers to feel proud and spur on growth.
1) In your work: _____ .
2) In your family life: _____ .
3) Past efforts: _____ .

Emerge resilient, show up with dignity, and serve up self-kudos. Say this mantra: *Validation is best from within.*

On the record: From this day forward, I will adopt a first-rate attitude. Welcome it in; open the door rather than slam it shut. Acknowledge even small victories and strive to create more.

To continue: I take responsibility for working through challenges. Creation of any masterpiece takes sweat equity.

In a Nutshell

* Walk with swagger—be proud of your accomplishments.

* Live with confidence—allow yourself to shine brightly.

* View life as a workout; exhibit a title holder's outlook.

Fight Complacency - Unlock Purpose

Complacency: The mark of precious time wasted.

_____

The Commitment

A challenge can be an exciting part of life. Reflect on this: Why make a compromise when you can make a commitment? Instead of accepting complacency because it's comfortable—get clear on what you value. There's no time like the present to live with purpose.

_____

Why put off a goal, dream, or desire? Make a promise and take action. I'm not saying to quit a job that supports your needs. If your aim is to work for yourself, why not begin by welcoming it as an enjoyable side hustle?

Create the time: Start engineering, lay your foundation, and proceed. Make the most of those free hours. Get off you duff —the clock doesn't stop for anyone!

2. *Tough love*: It's easy to be lulled into denial, believing you will do it eventually. Hesitating and making excuses widens the gap, making it harder to achieve. Say aloud—no more!

3. *Self-probe*: Why sit off to the side? Is a comfort zone *your* choice? It might be okay for some. Is that *your* final answer?

4. *Continue on*: It takes courage, spunk, self-determination, endurance, and guts. Settle or step up? Your truth will call out the reply.

It may not be for the faint of heart—risk brings hurdles and obstructions to vault over. Sometimes your footing may be unsteady. Dismiss that uneasy feeling—take a leap of faith.

 *Start Now:* **DITCH THE HABIT!**

> **Expose the truth: Have you been slacking? Who are you fooling? Disrupt complacency! Leave an honest voicemail for yourself prompting a call to action. Listen often and avoid wasting another second.**

The decision: Why hold on to bad habits that detract from personal growth? Instead, cultivate restorative time to amass energy for that shiny, new venture. Fight the urge to relapse into non-productive patterns. As discussed, having clarity, a plan to tackle tasks in bite-sized chunks, and a practice of celebrating wins can help fend off procrastination and stimulate progress.

> Picture this: When I think of sheer determination, I am motivated by Bethenny Frankel's dedication to succeed. Giving up wasn't an option. She has many credits: Culinary school, *Bethenny Bakes*, reality television, a national talk show, *Skinnygirl*, and the *Just B* podcast, to name a few. Frankel is also involved in philanthropy and is the founder of *BStrong*. She inspires me to step up and make a difference.

I repeat this mantra: *My someday is now!* Face the truth. Commit to those dreams. Own the power and bring them to life.

In a Nutshell

* Why make a compromise? Instead, make a commitment.

* Complacency doesn't look good on you; add discipline.

* Get off your duff, go around the obstruction. Do it now.

Become Who You Want To Be

Want to succeed? Add belief and courage. Once the mind is in sync, success is more likely to follow.

―――――――

The Commitment

Live your life with motivation. Quit standing in someone else's shadow. Don't be a follower—lead your way. Search deeply within yourself and passionately work on what you'd like to achieve.

―――――――

Why not be the best version of yourself?

Have you visited a secret, lofty daydream many times in your mind? Are you fearful or uncomfortable announcing your ambitions? Do you truly want to fulfill them?

Urgent request: What are you waiting for—your life to pass by? The time for excuses is over. Put your best foot forward. Think about what could materialize with action.

The saying goes: "If you want to get something done, ask a busy person." It's about commitment and desire.

A solution: Armed with organization, time management, and confidence, I harness the energy needed to not only see my ideas through, but also polish them to brilliance.

Repeating: What you are waiting for? The fork in the road leads either way. It's your decision which one to take.

 *Start Now*: **TAKE THE LEAP!**

How committed are you? Make a numbered chart detailing what's necessary to capture your dreams. List any changes or tweaks that will give you an edge.

Think about this: Have you heard of *Imposter Syndrome*? Do you feel like a phony or believe your accomplishments are due to luck rather than talent? If so, it's time to move past those feelings. Imagine lying on your deathbed and reflecting on what you didn't do. Allow that discomfort to be a call to action, and don't let anything stand in the way of a well-lived life.

1. *Self-challenge*: Apply your skills, dedication, and gifts to ignite the passions buried within. Prove that you're capable.

2. Perhaps a pinch of pressure or structure will tip the scales. Architect your future. If not now, when? If not you, who?

3. No more agonizing or stalling. It's time to step up. Draft the plan, put in effort, and build your road.

4. *Challenge continued*: Make the choice and work to craft a life according to your vision. Conscious living in action. The *New York Lottery* slogan says it all: "You gotta be in it to win it!"

My wager is on *you*. Share my mantra, reflect your commitment, and say with conviction: *I'm betting on myself.*

In a Nutshell

* Vow to become who you want to be. If not now, when?

* See your ideas through, then polish them to brilliance.

* Structure your time; shape your life—build your road.

Things To Remember:

Share an attitude of gratitude. Defend your dignity and honor your value. Guard your well-being! Don't be a scapegoat. Live a fulfilling life and paint it in your colors. Add the sunshine to light up today. Asking why helps guide the way. Altruism brings happiness, but rudeness doesn't. Acknowledge accomplishments and be proud of them. Stay humble, but always walk with confidence. Don't compromise away the years— fight complacency. Become who you want to be and polish yourself to brilliance. Sign the commitment.

* Live with gratitude. Be someone else's amazing angel.

* A daily rule: Never cause harm to anyone or yourself.

* Cherish life: Mix in self-love; step off the struggle bus.

* Life can be beautiful. Create today and own tomorrow.

* Muster up resilience. Ignite the light—give it your flair.

* Rise to the occasion—don't compromise your goals.

* Begin and end the day with positivity and appreciation.

* Strengths and achievements are fuel for future wins.

* Get off your duff: Unfriend complacency; live inspired.

* Walk with swagger! Be that person pictured in your mind.

Thoughts:

_____
_____
_____
_____
_____
_____
_____
_____
_____
_____
_____
_____
_____
_____
_____
_____
_____
_____
_____
_____
_____
_____
_____

Feel-Good Activity List: Visit thedailydecisions.com/inspire

In Closing

At ten years old, I was touched by the power of *intention manifestation*. I keep this memory close to my heart and mind.

During my first week at summer camp, while swimming in Lake Plunkett, I wore a silver ring with a tiger's eye stone that hid a secret compartment. It fell off my finger, disappearing into the water. My fear was that it was lost forever. Upset and hoping it would appear, that ring remained in my thoughts.

Two days before the end of camp, I dove down to the bottom of the lake, where my hand touched the wet sand, and I felt something. Yes, the ring! It was then that I first experienced what I had wished for might happen.

This ring has become a symbol, reminding me of those moments when I felt I had lost sight of my passions. By holding true to the dreams I cherished most, the courageous creator within me has always been present.

Our lives are works in progress. Make yours a successful, happy, and joyous journey for yourself and those who join in. Let your daily decisions complement your life's goals.

The time is now: Believe in yourself, stay positive, achieve your full potential, and never stagnate or limit yourself.

Connect With Deborah

I Look Forward To Having You Join My Community!

Receive Worksheets, Checklists, And Feel-Good Activities. They're Complimentary—Perfect Companions To This Book.

USE THE LINK OR SCAN THE QR CODE:

www.thedailydecisions.com/inspire

Invite me to speak at your next event!
email: info@thedailydecisions.com

I'd be grateful if you would:

Mention this book to anyone you know who'd benefit.

Write a review on the site used to purchase this book.

I would welcome your input on my next book.

Help me pick a title.

Use this link: thedailydecisions.com/book2

www.ingramcontent.com/pod-product-compliance
Lightning Source LLC
Chambersburg PA
CBHW061654120626
46550CB00003B/945